# The
# Melancholy Marriage

# The
# Melancholy Marriage

## Depression in Marriage and Psychosocial Approaches to Therapy

**Mary K. Hinchliffe**
*Mental Health Service*
*Bristol Health District*

**Douglas Hooper**
*Department of Mental Health*
*University of Bristol*

**F. John Roberts**
*Department of Psychological Medicine,*
*Wellington Clinical School, University of Otago*

## JOHN WILEY & SONS

Chichester · New York · Brisbane · Toronto

**Library of Congress Cataloging in Publication Data:**

Hinchliffe, Mary K.
  The melancholy marriage.

  Includes bibliographical references and index.
  1. Depression, Mental.   2. Marital psychotherapy.
I. Hooper, Douglas, joint author. II. Roberts, John, 1903–   joint author. III. Title.
RC537.H56        616.8'52        78–4526
ISBN 0 471 99650 5


Typeset by Computacomp (UK) Limited
Fort William, Scotland and printed by Unwin Brothers Ltd.,
The Gresham Press, Old Woking, Surrey.

# Contents

# FOREWORD

The authors of this book, who have all been members of the University of Bristol's Department of Mental Health, have each had lengthy experience of the techniques of psychotherapy with married couples. Psychiatrists, social workers and psychologists have worked as apprentices with them, and they have led many discussions in the Department on practice and theory. They are thoroughly familiar with the clinical aspects of the problems they have been researching. Readers who have themselves sat with a depressed person and spouse will appreciate the freshness of their clinical descriptions, which are illuminating and instructive.

They have adopted an interactional approach. That is, they regard the behaviour of a depressed person as both stimulus and response to the spouse's behaviour. The sequences of responses between them, which convey information and feelings, are governed by rules; these reflect the expectations each has of the other. The rules maintain a degree of consistency in the roles each plays, and put limits on their behaviour. Critical change in the pattern of their interaction comes about when there is a change in rules. Intervention by a therapist is one of the ways in which the rules can be changed.

The interactional approach is not new. H. S. Sullivan developed in the nineteen-thirties an 'interpersonal' theory of psychiatry as an alternative to psychoanalysis, with its emphasis on 'intrapsychic' processes. When during the second world war they took up the study of performance on skilled tasks, psychologists in the U.K., in Cambridge especially, broke away from the tradition regarding behaviour as reactive to situations; instead human operator and machine are seen as 'an interacting control system'. A similar development of ideas in North America led to the creation of a new branch of science, *cybernetics*, which later became incorporated into the more comprehensive *general system theory* Applications of the interactional approach in social psychology were pioneered by Gregory Bateson and his colleagues in Palo Alto, California; they studied interactional processes in schizophrenia especially, as did Sullivan before them. During the last few years, several groups with an interest in the psychotherapy of families have made use of concepts derived from general system theory.

The authors of this book are the first to make a resolute attempt to describe in detail the interactions of a depressed patient and spouse. They have come to grips with difficult problems. Notably, they have made systematic observations under controlled conditions, and have been able to make valid comparisons of the interactions of depressed patients and spouses before and after clinical recovery, depressed patients and strangers, and surgical patients and spouses. Their results define some of the complexities in the processes.

Taken altogether, their research justifies their modest claim that the interactional approach is a promising alternative to the medical approach of psychiatry, the intrapsychic approach of psychoanalysis, and the behavioural approach with its emphasis on differential learning because of reinforcement or the withholding of reinforcement. The interactional approach is complementary, not exclusive. It fills out the description of depressed patients by considering aspects not covered by the other approaches.

During the last decade there has been a progressive change in the way in which depressed patients are treated. The use of drugs has not been superseded, nor has E.C.T., but much more importance has been given to the involvement of the spouse, and sometimes other members of the family as well, in treatment. This book marks another step in this direction.

Derek Russell Davis
Professor of Mental Health
University of Bristol

# PREFACE

When the last word of the manuscript has been written, the authors can relax, take stock, and then look back at the past scenery which led them on to this creative peak and hope to describe for the reader what they now see from the top. What has happened to them (to continue the metaphor) is that they have been accompanied by the reader only for the ascent itself. The base work, the poring over the intellectual maps, the selection of the appropriate conceptual ropes, and all of the early climbs — these are the experiences in which the reader has played no part but which may give him important clues as to why this particular mountain was selected and why the climb has been accomplished in this way.

The real answers to these questions are hard to tease out from the more general web of experience and of course with three authors there are really three different sets of answers, but some of the strands are common to all of us and can be spelt out clearly. Over a period of some eight to ten years we have worked in various combinations of researchers, academics, and practising clinicians to think and feel about the puzzling nature of the experience of being depressed. When we began to think carefully about the issues involved the understanding of depression was still tied pretty heavily to ideas which were creaking at the joints, but now things are really very different. As we demonstrate in this book, there is a new spirit abroad with a tremendous ferment of new ideas and we want to contribute to that process.

Because there is such a flow of ideas now, we saw no need to continue the debates of decades in our own thinking. Thus the reader will find no mention for example of the question of the differential types of depressive disorder. We make no use of the notions of endogenous and reactive, neurotic and psychotic, or unipolar or bipolar depression. Partly this is because we feel these issues have occupied the stage for long enough, but more strongly because we feel that the approach we have adopted stands independently of this diagnostic biomedical approach. Finally, in the management and treatment of the vast majority of depressive problems they are relatively unimportant issues.

Our approach is unashamedly psychosocial and draws on sources which are not always a strong part of the British psychiatric scene. We have been fortunate in this way, since the Department of Mental Health at Bristol has been a congenial home for us and has not worried about developing a mildly deviant character as compared with other similar institutions. We were free to experiment with ideas and practices which might well have met with a more hostile response elsewhere, and for this our thanks go to Derek Russell Davis as Head of the Department. One of the most important roles which a University Department should play is to enable its members to go beyond the received wisdoms in its teaching practice and research, although this does not necessarily make it popular with full-time service colleagues.

We are also sure that we have each gained from being an interdisciplinary group, since two of us — John Roberts and Mary Hinchliffe — are psychiatrists and Douglas Hooper is a psychologist. This reflects the reality of our colleagues who are also an interdisciplinary group to which we attach considerable importance. There are always strong tendencies for professional groups to withdraw behind the walls of separatism and suspicion and these are processes which we strongly dislike.

Finally we should describe the way in which this book was written. Although it was conceived when we were all working together in Bristol, John Robert's removal to New Zealand made for a number of difficulties in the writing. In the event, all of us shared equally in the crucial preparation of the first drafts of chapters dividing the work amongst us. Then because of the problems of distance and time, Mary Hinchliffe and Douglas Hooper in consultation with John Roberts took on the responsibility for redrafting, reorganizing and rewriting the chapters. We trust that the reader will find that this process results in a reasonable smoothness in the reading.

Many people have shared in the work which has led to this book being written, but particular people have played an especial role. Clare Jones and Meredith Lancashire in the early years, and more recently Pamela Vaughan who was our research colleague when we were working on the material reported in Chapter V and we owe them our thanks for their contributions to our ideas. This segment of our work was also supported by a generous grant from the Nuffield Foundation and we would certainly wish to acknowledge the fillip which their support gave to our work. Lastly we should thank those who do the often thankless secretarial work. Our University secretary, Audrey Holliman, although she played no direct part in the production of the manuscript has contributed so much in innumerable other ways over the years, that her contribution is gratefully acknowledged by us. The pressures of the production of the final manuscript were shared by Mavis Hooper and Roseanne Morgan who met our final demands with great patience.

Bristol, England
Wellington, New Zealand      1977.

# 1

# DEPRESSION IN RELATION TO MARRIAGE

*... Let there be spaces in your togetherness*
*And let the winds of heaven dance between you.*
*Love one another, but make not a bond of love*
*Let it rather be a moving sea between the*
*shores of your souls*
*Fill each others cup — but drink not from one*
*cup,*
*Give one another of your bread; But eat not*
*from the same loaf*
*Sing and dance together and be joyous; But let*
*each one of you be alone*
*Even as the strings of a lute are alone, though*
*they quiver with the same music.*
*Give your hearts but not into each others*
*keeping*
*For only the hand of life can contain your*
*hearts*
*And stand together but not too near together*
*For the pillars of the temple stand apart,*
*And the oak trees and the cypress grow not in*
*each others shadow ...*

KAHLIL GIBRAN, THE PROPHET

The words of this poem draw out the intricate problems involved in establishing a satisfactory balance or equilibrium within an intimate relationship such as marriage. The balance of forces has to be nicely judged in order to deal with the individual's needs for feelings to be both given and received. It emphasizes the need to preserve individuality within the merger of a shared relationship and gives a warning about the dangers of over-involvement and over-dependence. The ingredients for a successful marriage are very varied and ultimately tend to relate to the idiosyncratic needs of the individuals concerned. Ideas about stereotyped male and female roles impose a rigid structure on our understanding and do not take account of the successful balance of forces in a specific relationship where roles are taken up to complement each other's needs.

The title of this chapter contains the two words which will pre-occupy us for the rest of this book and this first chapter attempts to tease out the meaning of these two words and discuss how they can be related together. They are both very evocative and describe profound areas of human experience which have been debated and described by innumerable writers over the centuries. But it is only very recently in human affairs that these two very different kinds of human experience have been studied in what we can think of as a broadly scientific way. Yet if we were concerned with that alone, this chapter could probably offer little that is new to the serious student of human behaviour. What we hope that this chapter and those that follow *will* do is to conjoin these two areas of behaviour in a way that will contribute something to both, but especially to the understanding of depression.

The reason for our differential hope is that in this account we shall discuss the important issue of the interpersonal nature of depression. This is a sharply different view from the one widely accepted by most mental health professionals, yet it enters so intimately into every aspect of therapeutic work that it is almost astonishing how much it has been taken for granted. So much so, that some of what we have to say will inevitably be speculative, albeit informed speculative thought based on reasonable extensions of some existing work. The emphasis will be on the nature of depression and marriage as human experiences rather than on depression as a clinical entity and marriage as a social institution.

We have written this book through the eyes of practising clinicians and therapists and therefore base our ideas on our own observations of human needs as witnessed through the lives of our depressed married patients. Therefore our intention is not to dissertate on the rightness of the present social institution of marriage, but rather to understand the human needs which have generated the formation of this social structure with its attendant rituals, rules and prohibitions. The patients who seek our help are generally ordinary folk with an inbred tolerance for traditional values and in our roles as therapists we do not see ourselves as justified in making value judgements about society's rules and mores where their marriages are concerned. We must accept the attitudes and values of our patients and work within the framework which they offer us. Thus we can accept a stable and enduring relationship which has not achieved the stamp and approval of society by passing through the ritual of the marriage ceremony, as possessing the same set of interactive and emotional needs as the legally contracted relationship.

Therefore we understand the institution of marriage as being society's answer to the individual's biological needs for pair bonding or attachment behaviour, a characteristic found throughout the animal world. The legal contract provides safeguards to ensure a secure base within which young may be reared and creates an opportunity for the human needs of mutual care, concern and affection to be expressed within the stability and security of a committed relationship.

Bowlby (1977) has drawn a distinction between dependency theory and attachment theory. He understands attachment behaviour in ethological terms as a biological feature of specific human relationships. Thus we are capable of exhibiting attachment behaviour at any stage of our lives from infancy to old age, and our early experiences in our relationships with our parents influence the pattern of this behaviour that we show later in life in marital and other relationships. We direct attachment behaviour exclusively to specific individuals and this pattern may persist for long periods of our lives. Bowlby emphasizes that the making, breaking and renewal of these close bonds of attachments involves an intense display of emotions. We fall in love, then we form a bond and 'continue loving' as we maintain that bond, and grieve when the bond is broken or disrupted. Similarly anxiety about the security of a bond gives rise to 'fear and anger', whereas 'security and joy' spring from the maintenance of a secure attachment.

Bowlby summarizes the situation by writing 'Because such emotions are usually a reflexion of the state of a person's affectional bonds, the psychology and psychopathology of emotion is found to be in large part the psychology and psychopathology of affectional bonds'. Dependent behaviour does not exhibit these characteristics, nor does it generate the same level of emotional involvement. We appreciate the dynamic qualities of this theory which links human emotions and biological needs with the emergence of psychologically disturbed behaviour. It offers a dynamic and interactive understanding for the emergence of grieving and depressed behaviour and sets it within the conceptual framework of anxieties and insecurities about the maintenance of affectional bonds in meaningful relationships such as parent — child or husband — wife.

In certain sectors of our modern society the institution of marriage is receiving a measure of criticism and rejection. The current emergence of the feminist movement expresses a mood of discontent with traditional values and demonstrates a growing need for an increasing appreciation of woman's role in society. In the past she has been relegated to wife and mother and this role has been equated with that of a second class citizen enslaved by her biological apparatus. This movement may represent a necessary revolution before male and female roles within the family can be re-evaluated and a greater measure of sharing and mutual freedom produced. However, it tends to minimize the importance of adult attachment behaviour and thereby denies the value of the emotional needs intrinsic in such a relationship.

Present dissatisfactions with the restraints of marriage are being increasingly revealed with the rising figures for divorce since the 1971 Divorce Law Reform Act.

DIVORCE AND REMARRIAGE (Office of Population Censuses and Surveys)

| | | 1961 | 1970 | 1971 | 1972 | 1973 | 1974 |
|---|---|---|---|---|---|---|---|
| Petitions filed (thousands) | | 31.9 | 71.7 | 110.9 | 110.7 | 115.5 | 131.7 |
| Decrees Absolute Rate/1000 Married Population | | 2.1 | 4.7 | 6.0 | 9.5 | 8.4 | 9.0 |
| Remarriages | | 14.6% | | 20.2% | 25.5% | 27.1% | 28.3% |
| Average Age of Marrying | M | 24.8 | (1974) | | | | |
| | F | 22.7 | | | | | |
| Average Age of Remarrying | M | 43.2 | (1974) | | | | |
| | F | 39.3 | | | | | |

Most people who do obtain a divorce do so in their late twenties and the commonest duration of a marriage ending in divorce is four years. But more than a fifth of the marriages that ended in 1975 had lasted more than 20 years. In spite of this high rate of marital breakdown remarriages of divorced people rose by 5% in 1975. About one in six of those marrying were divorced and the combination of two divorcees marrying has been increasing by about 7% annually.

The figures indicate the human need which motivates individuals once again to commit themselves to another civil contract with all its attendant potential pitfalls and limitations.

The binding quality of the legal contract seems to be important for the majority of people. One could suggest that it builds a further dimension of security into the attachment behaviour of two specific individuals.

The reasons for marital breakdown are complex and involve a range of factors from changing social expectations for greater fulfilment in our personal lives to the interpersonal problems which are the outcome of personality disturbances. Dominian (1972) has reviewed marital pathology and explored the many facets which contribute to breakdown. In a more recent survey of the personality characteristics of divorcees (from the Marriage Research Centre at Central Middlesex Hospital) he has demonstrated specific areas of interpersonal difficulty. Lack of involvement with the home was characterized by lack of interest in the children, preference for other activities away from home, and more extramarital relationships. In addition, an observed absence of warmth and affection was shown by more selfishness and meanness. Divorcees were described in general terms as less optimistic, more moody, less good tempered, more depressed, more of a show off, more jealous, more physically violent, more prone to drink heavily and also more lazy.

In an American study Briscoe and Smith (1973) have examined the part that depression plays both as a factor contributing to later divorce and also as a feature of the marital breakdown. Out of a group of 139 divorcees they found 45 depressives (33 female 12 male) and were able to break them down into two groups: those whose depressions were primarily associated with the marital breakdown and divorce (Event associated) and those who had suffered from depression at earlier stages in the marriage (Event non-associated). Of this second group 42% showed more previous psychiatric illness, more symptoms of panic and anxiety, and a more prominent family history of psychiatric illness.

In an interesting analysis of the incidence of depression in relation to the time of the divorce they were able to demonstrate the greater vulnerability of the female to depression in the period six months prior to the event (F 69% ; M 42%); a similar vulnerability for both sexes at the time of the event (F 88% ; M 83%) and a greater incidence for the male at the time of the final divorce proceedings (F 61% ; M 92%). These findings were borne out in an English study of 150 female divorce petitioners in Hull between 1967–70 (Chester, 1971). He described the associated morbidity which was temporally linked with the transition in marital status (latter period of marriage and early separation period). The research revealed that 101 of the women had consulted their G.P.s for a range of medicosocial disorders, the most common symptoms being weight changes, sleeping difficulties, changed smoking and drinking habits and self neglect.

Although the two studies mentioned here relate to the event of marital breakdown leading to divorce, they also clarify the pattern of psychological disturbance with which can occur when an attachment bond is severed and this need not be limited to an open declaration that a marriage has ceased. Anxieties and fears for the security of an intimate bond can lead to emotional detachment and alienation within a close relationship and can produce the same sequel of events. It is difficult to obtain statistics for degrees of marital breakdown as the partners may not seek help through the caring agencies for their problems. General Practice studies such as that of Shepherd, Cooper and coworkers (1966) reveal that marital problems feature as an important social factor in the etiology of psychological symptoms. They also found that significantly more women presented with marital problems than men and middle aged women predominated.

No doubt we have a 'tip of the iceberg' situation here and there may be a number of reasons why women consult their doctors more frequently for psychological symptoms than men do. They have more excuses to visit their G.P.s as a result of menstrual irregularities, family planning requirements, problems relating to their children and so on. In addition there seems to be less anxiety for women that they will 'lose face' by admitting the intimate details of their lives to an outsider. In general women tend to be more in touch with the emotional side of their lives than men do and have a greater capacity to make their emotional problems explicit. No doubt the male has a greater opportunity to find support and companionship at work and divides his life more completely between the home and work situations. This may reduce the pressure for him to seek specific help. It is also socially acceptable for him to seek solace in his friendly neighbourhood pub and alcohol may feature as a regular tranquillizer.

Studies of attempted suicide cases have also revealed the high incidence of marital problems which lie behind the act. In our own study of 100 consecutive cases (Roberts and Hooper 1969), we found that most of them could be understood if the patients interactions with others in their environment were considered. We found that the spouses of the depressed patients were not just the 'fit' partner, but were also disturbed in some way. We rarely found as did Harrower (in Eisenstein and coworkers, 1956) 'that the least disturbed partner comes to treatment first'. As most of the patients were married, this led to our increased interest in the role of marriage itself.

Many other studies of a range of types of psychological and psychiatric disturbance show that those who are unmarried are particularly at risk from a psychiatric point of view, but where depression is concerned the reverse is true. We will discuss the evidence for this in Chapter 3.

We have now made a case for the interactional basis for depressive symptoms within a disturbed marriage, whether it be at the time of a major breakdown of marriage or not. However at this point we will digress in order to explain our own understanding of depression itself.

## Depression and its Meaning

The everyday usage of the word 'depression' and the psychiatric usage share much common ground. The psychiatrist and psychologist have attempted to limit the meaning by providing operational definitions, whereas the man-in-the-street is content with a series of synonyms to explain what depression means. Yet although the clinician has a vocabulary for talking about the mental state, the feeling, and the clinical condition, he is without words when he tries to talk about processes, interaction and the patterns of communication in relationships. Even Eisenstein and his colleagues (1956) in discussing the general issue of neurosis in marriage had available to them a whole range of ideas, including General Systems Theory, and yet the nearest they got to a truly interactional account was to describe the individual psychopathologies and characteristics of the couple and then to comment on them in terms of one individual's compatibility or congruence with the other.

There are two main reasons why we find it difficult to move into a new area and escape from the restrictions of familiar language, quite apart from the fact that we may have to develop a new vocabulary. First, up until the present time any talk about depression has depended on words which are concerned with an individual person or thing, and they do not transfer easily to the new way of thinking. In practice this means that when we start to talk about depression, a whole range of familiar words come to mind and do not transfer to an interactive vocabulary. Secondly we require a new conceptual model, or a new root metaphor in Popper's terms (1942). By metaphor we mean a linguistic device which seeks to enlighten one idea with another which is borrowed from a second or unrelated source. For the interested reader we have included an appendix which examines the models and metaphors which have been used over the centuries to clarify our understanding of depression.

The scientist has attempted to limit the use of the word depression to an operationally defined clinical condition. However in everyday usage the term may be used both as a noun and a metaphor as well as applied to a syndrome, disease, mood or process!

During the nineteenth century the word depression began to supersede the two more poetic words 'melancholia' and 'melancholy'. Depression was invariably used as part of a metaphorical expression so that 'his mind is depressed' of 'there is depression of spirits', are typical of the way in which the word and its derivatives were used. At the turn of the century, partly because of the recommendation of Adolf Meyer (1905) depression, shorn of its metaphorical phrases, began to replace the term melancholia in medical and psychological writings. Presumably, it was because of the idea contained in the word of something being lowered or below normal, that made it so attractive and acceptable.

There are actually a group of words which are frequently used in association with depression or as synonyms for it and with the exception of a small number they have as their reference point part or all of the body. 'Heavy', 'tired' and 'low' clearly refer to the individual's body and although the implication of 'dejected' is that it is used about the feelings or spirits, its literal meaning is thrown down. In a similar way, 'despondent' is used about feelings but it is derived from a French expression which is best translated as 'to lose heart'; the everyday English equivalent would be 'to give up'. There are many other expressions which refer to the heart in the context of depression such as 'heavy' or 'sinking' heart and an African tribe use the picturesque phrase 'my heart is in a wooden box'.

The everyday expression 'fed-up' continues the body reference with the metaphorical notion of being stuffed with food to an unacceptable extent to that it is very uncomfortable. It is interesting to note that the etymology of 'sad' is virtually the same as 'satiate' and 'satisfy' — which of course are synonyms of 'fed-up'. In certain parts of England 'sad' is used as a colloquial description for cake or pastry which is baked but has not risen to the expected extent.

Some words, while retaining the body as their referent, also imply that the environment is perceived as the cause of the condition, while others that it is perceived by the individual as different from the normal. 'Despair' is such a word which is derived from a source which means to be without hope. Although at first sight 'hope' is not a word which we readily associate with the body, according to Partridge (1966) hope comes from the same root as 'hop' and therefore 'to hope' is to feel that it is possible to hop or leap forward expectantly. In part, therefore, to hope is to assume that there is a way forward, or to respond to the perception of a way forward. The converse, when in despair, is to be hopeless. Both 'lousy' and 'miserable' are indirect body-referent words. The former is self-explanatory, although today it is much more likely to be used in a metaphorical rather than literal way. 'Miserable' and 'misery' are both to do with the state which once resulted from environmental privation and poverty although again, it is in the metaphorical form that we most often encounter them now.

'Hopelessness', 'despair', 'lousy' and 'miserable' draw attention to the relationship of the depressed person to his environment. The articulate depressed person will often also struggle to put into words the fact that not only does there appear to be no way forward and thus no point to life — but that the world actually looks different. This may be expressed in very general terms, but at times this is put quite specifically — as did Coleridge in his *Ode to Dejection* when he wrote:

> I see them all so excellently fair —
> I see, not feel, how beautiful they are!

Another word 'desolate' emphasizes the solitary egocentric nature of the depressive's experience. It concerns itself in meaning exclusively with the reality and form of the relationship of an individual to others. There is an intense pre-occupation with self shown by many depressed people and it is not surprising that the descriptive language should be focussed on the individual. However, there is either a remarkable lack of language to deal with the interpersonal experiences which are so much part of the phenomenon, or the perceptual bias which provokes a sense of guilt and low self-esteem, blinds the sufferer, and prevents him from clarifying and verbalising the interactive aspects of the experience.

So much for descriptive words but how do we view the so-called clinical state of 'depression'? We do not understand psychological symptoms as descriptive of underlying pathology as one sees in general medical terms. Although we do not deny the importance of such symptoms as weight loss, reduced appetite, diminished less and the so-called vegetative symptoms of depression, we do affective mood changes as serving a communicative function. They s' means of self-expression, their only way of impressing on others in ment their needs and feelings. Thus they have a demand quality and in al terms are searching for an appropriate response in others around them. iscuss in later chapters how variable this demand quality can be from one situ n to another and the associated hostility which can be demonstrated in intimate relationships compared with non-intimate ones. McPartland and Hornstra (1964) describe the severity of the depressive experience in interactive terms. They see depressed individuals ranged along a continuum of increasing stridency in terms of their capacity to communicate with the external world. They write:

> 'Patients who are farthest along this dimension, whose communication is most diffuse, non-specific, strident and unanswerable are likely to have had long histories of psychiatric illness. We find that the more unanswerable messages come from people whose life spaces are the most disrupted and whose lack of an involved audience is greatest.'

The messages themselves they see as commencing with oblique indications of withdrawal from social interaction by slowing, irritability, or agitation. Those to whom the messages are directed thus have a burden thrust on them for some kind of initiative largely because of the obliqueness of the message. More strident are the messages which tell of hopelessness and helplessness, progressing on to lowered vitality and a decrease in ability to perform ordinary everyday social obligations. Implicit in these messages is the notion of a stalemate. Beyond this is the stage in which the social relations are more clearly disrupted with messages of worthlessness, badness and evil. Finally, there are the most strident messages of all, which are so diffuse and incomprehensible that they acquire the label of psychotic. These authors suggest that the messages are at first directed to quite specific individuals, but that as the depressive process develops the audience becomes more and more undifferentiated and diffuse.

Marriage, or a longstanding partnership occupies the major part of our lives and therefore forms a focus for interpersonal problems and difficulties in adjustments to others needs. Anthony Ryle (1974) expresses this in conceptual terms from his analysis of married dyads using the Repertory Grid.

> 'For most adults marriage is the most intense and long continuing social process experienced and one which would seem to offer the most opportunity to extend the accurate construction of the other; one also which one would expect to extract the highest price for failure to do so accurately.'

In this description he touches on the ongoing interactive process of marriage and suggests that there is an opportunity and an option whether the individual gives and gains a maximum of gratifying experience through the intimacy of the relationship or whether by failing to do so they only reap dissatisfaction and misery.

We have developed our notion of the communicative value of depressed behaviour and have put it within the framework of marital dissatisfactions and disturbances. The affectional bonding experience which marriage offers is of central importance for our own individual development and maturation. It offers the opportunity and potential for achieving personal fulfillment and gratification. If the relationship fails in some way to provide for these needs the outcome can be the depressive experience of isolation, misery and despair.

## Systems Theory

We propose now to use a different conceptual framework in order to express these ideas in a more technical language so that a more exact scientific interpretation and understanding can be gained.

Sullivan (1953) and the Neo-Freudians made the first moves in the direction of understanding individuals within their social environment. The underlying theme was the individual's search for 'security and satisfaction' in human relationships. This led to Sullivan's 'Theory of Reciprocal Emotion' where he understood the 'complementary needs of one person to articulate with the needs of another'. At the same time he defined the properties and dynamic characteristics of the 'Self System' whose basic function is to retain an inner stability by avoiding anxiety.

The development of General Systems Theory by Von Bertalanffy in the 1940s offered an all-embracing monistic theory which included the biological and emotional, as well as the social, economic and cultural aspects of life. It was an approach which could include the old ideas of biology and psychology as well as newly gained data from modern fields of endeavour such as sociology, ethology, cybernetics and communications theory. Meir (1969) discusses its use and application in Medicine and Psychiatry.

We can understand a system as being a component in a network of interacting parts which are interdependent on each other and yet are individually unique and whole within themselves. They are organised into a heirachy of supra-systems and sub-systems so that each system is Janus-faced (double-faced) (Koestler, 1964). One facet relates to supra-systems above in the heirachy and the other facet to sub-systems below. The total system is whole and complete within itself and is not equivalent to the sum of the individual parts contained within it. The attributes or characteristics of the component parts offer the potential for a new level of function which is produced as a result of the product of the transactions between individual parts. This concept is described as non-summativity. The individual system has specific primary activity which is innate and independent of outside activity. It also has inherent potential for its own development which may depend on specific conditions in its environment and this is the principle of equifinality. For example one individual may have the innate potential to feel love and affection for another person, but the attribute will not be developed in the absence of an appropriate other person.

Biological and human systems are described as open systems. This indicates that they exchange energy with their environment, yet their component parts remain constantly in flux and they remain whole and distinct as an entity. However they are able to vary their level of functioning according to external influences in the same way as an organism does when it changes through growth. Thus the component parts remain in a steady but not static state, and the system is able to maintain an inner equilibrium or homeostasis through negative feed back or cybernetic mechanisms.

Menninger (1963) links psychoanalytic theory with Systems Theory and understands the 'ego' to act as the cybernetic feedback and describes it as having a signal function (like a governor) between instinctual drives and reality. The ego uses devices such as suppression, repression, sublimation, taking flight, identifying with the enemy etc., in order to maintain a steady state for the organism.

> 'The ego may be described as a controlling agency which recognises, receives, stores, discriminates, integrates and acts by restraining, releasing, modifying and directing impulses. ..'

Thus the ego is the guardian of the 'vital balance.'

## The Marital System

We will now apply this set of ideas to the dyadic relationship of marriage and follow through the process which leads to the emergence of depression from within this system.

The husband and wife can be understood in simple terms, as two component parts of a system which individually bring their own set of characteristics or attributes to the system. The marital system does not represent the sum of their individual contributions, but becomes the result of the new level of functioning which they achieve through their transactions (non summativity).

$$(H) + (W) = \left( (H) \; (W) \right) \quad \text{New System}$$

Their newly-formed system has the potential for growth, change and creativity as the two individuals make a unique dyadic combination through their opportunity to encourage, support and complement each other's needs and skills. If the newly-formed system fails to develop its potential and show growth to new functioning levels it may become unstable. Then confusing, contradictory and destructive needs may disturb the functioning level and render it unstable. In order to re-establish a new equilibrium the system produces behavioural symptoms of strain and stress. These symptoms can include a range of psychological patterns indicating the system's need to defend itself against external or internal influences in the way that Menninger has suggested. However we are concerned for the emergence of depressed behaviour as a symptom of system disequilibrium. It is a symptom which emerges when affective needs are unacknowledged or misinterpreted in one way or another, and therefore arises from within the system and continues to be carried or sustained by the altered level of homeostasis developed by the system.

As soon as we plunge into a world of the technical language of biophysics and the computer we tend to dehumanise the implicit human experience which underlies our discussion. We are in an area where an appropriate descriptive language becomes a problem. In order to describe further interactive dynamics in terms of human communication we have drawn heavily from the theoretical approaches and language of Watzlawick and coworkers (1968) and also Raush and coworkers (1974). In order to understand the ongoing dynamics of the interaction we are striving to find a means whereby we can freeze an interactive event and translate its communicative significance in a frame by frame analysis of its sequence and transpose this information into a meaningful dialogue.

In human terms we understand the transactions between members of the marital systems as being different forms and levels of communication. Interaction is concerned with the flow of information between two systems and information relates to the surprise value of the event in System H that will influence System W. Thus if there is an event in System H which may for example reinforce the verbal content of the message such as sudden laughter or anger, then there will be a greater exchange of information. If we put this into human terms we can say that the husband's attempts to transmit information to his wife will depend on *his* ability to influence *her* existing responsiveness in such a way that *he* facilitates or inhibits *her* response to *his* message. Or to use another technical term we can say that his piece of behaviour may limit or constrain her behaviour. At the same time the communication process is a circular dynamic one which is being constantly self-modified and self-limited by means of feedback processes. Thus the husband must continually monitor each minute response which he views in his wife and adapt his next sequence of behaviour appropriately in order to reduce the anxiety which exists between two people attempting to give and receive a communication. Similarly his wife is synchronously modifying *her* responses in order to decode the moment by moment information which her husband transmits. Failure to adjust and adapt to the continually changing pattern of communication by a rigidity or avoidance of response leads to alienation of the two partners and may produce a further attempt to communicate by second order strategies which manipulate the relationship.

Constraints or limitations may be thought of as rules or messages about communication (meta-communication). They control the way in which information is received and may therefore enhance or diminish the communication. Some constraints are contextual variables or givens e.g. the sex of the individual giving the message, or the length of the marriage, or the repetitive nature of the message, and prior knowledge of each others ideas and attitudes; others relate to the idiosyncratic style of communication of a particular couple where distinctive control methods or 'games' may be evolved. Another important constraint which influences the effectiveness of communication is the mood of both the sender and the recipient. We see depression as influencing the capacity a couple have for relaying a message and also for affecting the message quality which is finally received. We are therefore understanding the very strongly-toned and negatively expressed messages which are so common in the style of depressed people, as constraints, or controls, which

*dynamics of gettin pissed off*

regulate a communication sequence. It is important to emphasise that it is these very communicative acts which the clinician describes as the 'symptoms' of depression. Taking our reasoning a stage further, we can say that symptoms emerge within a sequence of communication in order to direct and control the way a message is received and understood. In our earlier discussion of system homeostasis we emphasized the need for a system which has become unstable to re-establish a new order of equilibrium. We understand depressive symptoms as emerging to fulfil this function. Thus stress applied to a system, whether it be applied internally from personality conflicts, or externally from other pressures and influences, can disturb the systems equilibrium to such an extent that new constraints in the form of depressive symptoms emerge to reset the equilibrium at a level where one partner takes on the rôle of patient.

A new pattern of relationships then develops where the patient/partner becomes justified in making more overt demands and is given an excuse to opt out of certain front line responsibilities and slide into a helpless dependency. The so-called 'fit' partner may then direct his or her tensions and anxieties into assuming a caring role or into avoiding intimate contact and thereby increasing the sense of remoteness and distance from someone who causes confusion, and bewilderment in the relationship. On each side, however, a new set of rigid rules become imposed on an unstable situation which brings a new sense of order and control to their problems.

We can further elaborate on the message quality of symptoms when we understand that they carry two levels of communication — the verbal information which is relayed in the words used (the digital mode in computer terms) and the representational information which is communicated by a repertoire of non-verbal cues (the analogic mode). When symptoms indicative of psychological distress are produced they invariably carry a confusion in their message quality and this is especially true of depressive symptoms. For example, weeping can be a powerful real communication and indicates that the weeper feels precisely as he or she looks — dejected and miserable. However, at a verbal level the individual gives a different message of feeling helpless worthless and inadequate and needing to be utterly dependent. It is easy for the partner to respond to the message quality of the tears, but he or she rapidly learns that reassurances at a verbal level will not be accepted and repeated demands for continued assurances indicate the patient's underlying rejection of any help which is being offered. The spouse rapidly becomes frustrated by the verbal demands which he or she cannot meet and a situation develops which is ripe for a sequence of pathological communication to occur. So then the communication becomes either avoided or if accepted is rapidly disqualified or rejected. This easily leads on to emotional non-involvement or alienation which will be experienced by the depressed person as rejection of their concept of self, which then simply intensifies the communication experience. The depressive rule now becomes firmly built into further communication, which is then likely to affect the whole system and increasing non-communication leads the sufferer to the point of withdrawing completely into a state of retarded apathy. McPartland and Hornstra (1964) have a most evocative phrase to describe this state of affairs when they say that the communicative sequences have now become 'interactive blind alleys or stalemates in the dialogue of living'. We will discuss the nature of this stalemate in more detail in Chapter 7 dealing with the depressive's relationship with his/her family. We can say that the emotional ambivalence of the patient becomes the major rule of the communication, and thus destroys the sequencing, giving rise to a build up of hostility and tension which may manifest itself in despairingly aggressive outbursts directed both towards themselves and to others.

Perhaps we can illustrate these dynamics more clearly by examining a case history.

A young married woman in her early thirties was referred to the clinic with recurrent depression and an obsessional pre-occupation with cleanliness and germs which meant that she found it impossible to travel into the centre of cities and insisted on being interviewed in a clinic in a green belt area. It was significant that she arrived without her husband, having been escorted in the car by her mother and her daughter (her only child). Her husband had taken her already for a series of private consultations with different psychiatrists and clearly saw the problem as being confined to his wife.

She complained of feeling depressed and miserable for the preceding two to three years, which seemed to relate to her daughter's entry to school. She admitted to separation anxieties and this had become abnormally exaggerated when her daughter had been offered a booster polio immunisation at her first school. She then became aware of an overwhelming pre-occupation with infection and germs in relation to her daughter. She refused the offer of immunisation and then surrounded her daughter with lavish care and protection, fearing that any visits to centres of population for any family member might infect her.

There had always existed a tug-of-war situation between the two sets of grandparents, both husband and wife being spoilt and infantilised by their parents and in particular by their mothers. The situation had suddenly become more precarious two years before when the husband had inherited the family grocer's business folowing his father's death and at the same time had found himself taking responsibility for his mother, who lived over the shop. The husband's response to the increased demands which were being made on him was to become increasingly remote from his wife and to spend more and more time pre-occupied with his business, permitting his mother to take over a caring role in relation to him. The wife for her part increased her dependency within both the relationship with her mother and her daughter. Her depressive symptoms and obsessional pre-occupations confused and alienated her husband. He responded to her obvious distress by spending money on private treatment, but rejected her ambivalent emotional demand by retreating from her.

He continued to express this ambivalence in treatment and agreed to come in his role as an informant about his wife's problems, but jibbed repeatedly with minor excuses when an attempt was made to draw him into marital therapy. Eventually he let go of his hostile rejecting behaviour and began to understand the poor quality of their communication and increased his sense of awareness for the underlying affection in their relationship, and re-ordered his sense of personal priorities in life. Once he had re-orientated in this way the wife began to respond by reducing her tensions, obsessional pre-occupations and gradually freeing her daughter. She began to feel appreciated and valued and the depressive symptoms disappeared and she was able to take a more responsible role both in their home and in the family business.

We can understand the wife's depressive and obsessional symptoms as a constraint or control within the marriage. She became considered as the sick person in the household which made a demand on her husband to be a more caring person. He dealt with this demand by spending money on her and taking her to many doctors for treatment. However he experienced difficulty in responding to the other demand for more closeness and understanding because of his wife's repetitive childish obsessional behaviour and her depressive pre-occupations, which led at times to stormy tantrums. He found this second level of demand totally confusing and found it easier to disengage and avoid her at an intimate level and attempt to buy his way out of the problem. As time passed the interpersonal tensions increased to such an extent that an 'interactive stalemate' became established and both became locked in their new roles and experienced considerable difficulty in re-establishing a more effective level of intimate communication. This case history emphasizes the importance of viewing the patient's problem within the context of the marriage and the family. It would have been all too easy to collude with this husband and subject the wife to a range of antidepressant medication and when progress became a problem rationalize the situation by reasoning that obsessional symptoms can be notoriously difficult to treat and this woman had slipped into a chronically depressed posture.

One can argue that to see one partner alone represents the examination of only one unit of the dyadic marital system. It is always fascinating in clinical work to appreciate how differently two people conceptualise one relationship. Their view of each other's behaviour is so biased by their own needs and expectations for marriage that it is very easy for one or both to slip into a persecuted position where a partner's lack of response or withdrawal is interpreted as hostile, threatening and aggressive behaviour.

**Marital Systems applied to Roles and Thematic Games**

The roles which husband and wife define for themselves within marriage can be many and varied. They are idiosyncratic to the couple and are dependent on their cultural backgrounds and expectations for role responsibilities in marriage and they are subject to redefinition at different stages and for changing needs within the marriage.

The purpose of a well-defined role is to enable the other partner to play out a suitable complementary role so that the marriage as a whole can function. Because of the reciprocal nature of the roles within a close relationship like marriage, it is possible to think of the rules which govern the role set for adequate performance.

These 'rules' are true system properties in that they can only be used when the couple is together and rely on an adequate role set. They can be both idiosyncratic to the couple and also sufficiently general in pattern to enable one marriage to be compared with another. When these rules are put together with roles in a marriage, it is possible to conceptualise the resulting structure as a *thematic game* which extends over a long period of time but which handles interpersonal problems within the marriage. It is then possible to see a depressive response as just such a pathological thematic game.

Other writers and notably Berne (1964) have analysed and described at length the thematic games of neurotic relationships and probably come nearest to depressive games in 'kick me' and 'ain't it awful'. One can see the development of new roles, or the redefinition of old ones, in terms of altered rules or constraints within the relationship. As the system finds a new equilibrium so the role relationships will change.

One of us (Roberts, 1971) used this form of analysis in the detailed study of a couple where the marriage had worked well while they played the symmetrical roles of husband and wife, but when the wife became pregnant she became intent on assuming the role of mother to the exclusion of her wife role. Her husband redefined his role and related to her more as a son and found relief from his depressive feelings and the relationship became more stable for a time. However after her delivery his wife gradually viewed this change as a profoundly unsatisfactory situation for her and struggled to redefine her role as wife again. As she did so she in turn became depressed.

During treatment they were able to understand that they were dealing with the anxieties of the changing needs in their relationship by assuming a marked complementarity of roles which was highly gratifying to both of them. The game warded off negative feelings and established a new level of stability within their relationship. However other complexities within the relationship threatened this newly established role stability and they reverted to an unsatisfactory symmetrical role relationship which was once again associated with the emergence of depressive symptoms.

Lederer and Jackson (1968) have analysed these thematic games in some detail in order to be able to compare marriages. They have found that the use of two dimensions enables an effective classification to be made, and the two dimensions are stability–instability and satisfaction–dissatisfaction. They then combine each pole of the dimension with another yielding a four-fold classification namely;

| | |
|---|---|
| stable–satisfactory | unstable–satisfactory |
| stable–unsatisfactory | unstable–unsatisfactory |

The ordinary observer often finds such a scheme perplexing because he cannot see how a marriage which is unsatisfactory can be stable — and vice-versa. But it is precisely these arrangements which the thematic game allows. The characteristics of each type are interesting although there are also variants within the type. The stable–satisfactory marriages are based on a high degree of trust between individuals who come from similar and stable backgrounds and where collaboration is important and effective. Unstable–satisfactory pairs are those in which the relationship is constantly shifting the power from one partner to another, but not in a way which is necessarily destructive.

The stable–unsatisfactory type is almost the reverse in that the couple often insist on the stability of their marriage without being able to offer any evidence that it is rewarding. The authors say that in 'their quiet socially respectable manner' these couples suffer pain, hate deeply, and cause much discomfort to others without being aware of their behaviour. The contrast with the last group of the unstable–unsatisfactory is that although these, too, are often stable in the sense of continuing to exist, the theme is one of complaint and conflict. Lederer and Jackson put the chronic psychosomatic husbands and wives in this category and suggest that they handle both the instability and the dissatisfaction through their unremitting symptoms.

The theme is likely to vary considerably within each type and will depend upon the life of each partner. This means that the marriages have a private quality which has to be revealed by the couple or uncovered by the observer before the associated game can be seen. In the pathological pairs the roles within the theme are likely to be quite rigid but also highly predictable, which thus ensures that there is still some stability within the whole marriage, despite all the problems. We have already discussed the fact that the depressive response may well emerge when the game goes wrong and the pay-off is disproportionately distributed to the disadvantage of one of the pair.

## The Interactional Model of Depression

Earlier in this chapter we referred to the number of metaphors and 'models' which have been created in order to help in the understanding of depression. The emphasis in this book is on the interactional model, which is a new addition to a much more ancient group of models. These are described in greater detail in Appendix I, but we need to draw attention here to the organizational model of depression which is the real precursor to the one we are developing. This model of depression presupposes a complex arrangement of processes inside the psyche of the individual and uses a variety of metaphors to describe the nature of the processes.

Psychologists and psychologically-minded psychiatrists have worked largely with the organisational model theories and it is these which have achieved considerable complexity. They certainly do justice to a good deal of the experience of the depressed person, but it is still very surprising that the shift to an interactional model did not begin to take place until very recently. Yet there was no lack of experience to account for this quite startling omission, but rather simply the incapacity to jump the gap as it were. Once an observer is safe on the interactional side of the intellectual crevasse (to coin another metaphor!) then the phenomena reveal themselves in quite different ways.

Although there has been a plethora of study and research which has focused on the interactional problems of marriage, little has been written until recently which has embraced the affective aspects of the interactive experience. Two recent studies of Brown and his colleagues (1975) and Weissman and Paykel (1974) have specifically focussed on the interpersonal problems of depressed women. Brown and coworkers (1975) have highlighted the important quality that a good intimate relationship offers where the married woman is concerned. This supports our notion of the importance of establishing effective attachment behaviour between couples if the relationship is to be fulfilled in a creative supportive sense. The American study of Weissman and Paykel has examined some interactional features of the depressed woman's marriage both at the time when she is severely depressed and at recovery some eight months later. In particular they illustrated the damaging effects of the hostility and friction which becomes a feature of interpersonal relationships in her immediate intimate family group. They discussed the continued difficulty which these women demonstrated in interpersonal relationships after recovery from the depressive symptomatology and questioned whether this was a feature of their pre-depressive relationship or was the end result of a depressive experience. We will refer to other features of these studies in later chapters.

We have carried out our own research study based on the interactional model we have suggested. Our object was to analyse the communication between husband and wife where one partner was labelled as a depressed in-patient and we compared 20 such couples with a group of Surgical control couples.

We found marked differences in the expressive style of depressed men compared with depressed women and in each interaction were able to demonstrate the interactive role of the non-depressed partner. The male patients exhibited high levels of tension and hostility when they were depressed and this was mirrored by their wives' tense, anxious behaviour at this time. However, by 'recovery' most of these men had made a 'dramatic' change and once again this was mirrored by their wives' more relaxed behaviour and an easier style of interaction was observed. The depressed women showed a pattern more like that found by Weissman and Paykel. They and their husbands demonstrated tense, anxious, hostile behaviour when the wives were clinically depressed and this form of interaction persisted in large measure when the wives were considered to be recovered. In comparison the control couples' behaviour was characterized by a relaxed, playful, teasing style of interaction associated with a confidence in challenging and confronting each other and becoming conciliatory when the need arose.

We formulated some of our findings in terms of roles and found this a useful conceptualisation since it carried an interactive connotation. We suggested that since the male tends to be more instrumental in his orientation, the switch to a more expressive, dependent role which accompanies the depressive posture may be less tolerable for him than for the expressively orientated female. This may then motivate him to reject this role more rapidly than the female counterpart who is experiencing an enhancement of her controls within the marriage and has less need to revert back to her more responsible 'fit' role. We develop these ideas in detail in Chapter 4.

The reader may argue that these patterns of tension and hostility are a feature of any marriage in conflict and do not apply exclusively in depression. We would certainly agree that inter-role conflict is a feature of any marriage under strain and one can witness a varied repertoire of responses which are idiosyncratic to individual marriages. However our argument supports the theoretical view which we have postulated for the development of depressive behaviour in particular.

We have given our reasons for seeing married partners as being the interactants whom we wish to study. But we are not for one moment denying that depression is reserved solely for the married, and the set of ideas which we are setting out here and which is developed in the rest of the book could be usefully applied to other role sets. The fact remains that the vast bulk of people who become depressed are married or recently have been, or are in some similar stable relationship. We therefore needed to develop our ideas about the nature of marriage and this was done in the context of General Systems Theory. Two important aspects of the Systems idea which apply particularly to marriages are those of theme and game — thematic game. It may again be worthwhile repeating that word game here is itself used in a metaphorical sense and does not carry the notion of lightheartedness which it may appear to imply. Some writers have in fact used the idea in that way so that it becomes a party trick for someone to identify your marital game. As far as we are concerned if it is to carry some epithet, it should be that of the deadly serious marital game.

Finally we have need of a much finer focus for understanding the fascinating detail of the married pair in the pathology of depression and for this purpose have suggested that the concept of communication is very important. This may well prove to be the most important aspect of the new metaphor because it somehow has the 'feel' of the living process about it. But more than this, it is a very new approach to some of the major problems of human behaviour. For these reasons it is not necessarily easy to integrate with the older forms of understanding of depressive phenomena. Indeed such an integration may really be impossible.

With the main elements of the interactional model now spelled out clearly, the rest of the book develops each idea in greater detail by applying these in turn to the observations by ourselves and others in the exploratory and therapeutic spheres.

# 2

# MARITAL ROLES AND DEPRESSION

One of the most important organizing concepts in the last chapter was that of role, and role structure. The interactional model which we have proposed relies upon this concept (or set of concepts) quite heavily and this chapter will be devoted to an examination of roles both theoretically and practically. We feel that the role concepts are important, both in terms of understanding many of the depressive phenomena, but also in enabling us to work out useful therapeutic strategies. Indeed it is obvious that if the model of depressive behaviour which we offer has any virtue, the model must include the use of role theory in therapeutic work with patients and their spouses.

Role concepts have of course been widely used by a variety of workers in seeking to explain disordered behaviour but they have not (to our knowledge) been used before in trying to understand depression. However, where they have been used, they have mostly been seen as relatively static and as part of formal social structural types of explanation and not used to describe dynamically the interpersonal process themselves. For example, Scheff (1966) produced a brilliant description of the ascription of generalized social roles to people exhibiting various kinds of psychological disorder, but it was necessarily at a level of very broad social abstraction in order to demonstrate the range of the factors which could be invoked. At this level the concept of 'role' is almost light years away from the small-scale level of the individual marriage which we are working at and hence the reader needs to bear in mind that with such an apparently hard-working and useful concept as role there is the real danger of confusion between levels which may be more familiar, and the level of ideas which will be developed in this chapter.

The first step is to define the concept 'role' and then to discuss some of the theoretical reasons for seeing it as an organizing framework for much of the subsequent discussion. The conceptual approach which we shall use will draw heavily on the work of Biddle and Thomas (1966) who have worked out in considerable detail the set of ideas which have become associated with the role as an organizing principle. In defining the concept of these roles these authors limit the word itself to a fairly narrow range of phenomena which they say is supported by many others writers even though there are disagreements over more subtle aspects of the idea. They write: 'It is impossible to capture the diversity and complexity of the person–behaviour matrix with a single concept such as role [and] ... the question naturally arises as to whether the word 'role' should be abandoned altogether. We think not, provided that the word is employed only by itself to denote the generic idea of the particular behaviour of given persons, i.e. to refer to the entire person–behaviour matrix, and provided that more specific concepts are used when speaking of given segments of the matrix.' (Biddle and Thomas, 1966, p. 31)

By the 'person–behaviour matrix' they are referring to the intersection of two separate concepts which together form the matrix. The first of these is the 'behavioural class set' which refers to the set of behaviour which relates to specific spatio-temporal settings. A simple example of this would be the behaviour associated with traffic direction at a busy intersection. In addition this behaviour also belongs to what they call in their second concept the 'subject set' which in this case may be one or many individuals. In our example the subject set is that of traffic police and in one particular setting one particular policeman. This obviously excludes the generalised use of the word role unless it is qualified in terms of these two aspects of the matrix.

The matrices with which we are particularly concerned are those which are interpersonal and the writers go on to define role for these settings. Here the concepts which are particularly useful to us are those of *individual role* (which is how A actually behaves), *aggregate role* (which is the totality of the individual roles), and the reciprocally related *behaver* and *target* roles. The first of these is the behaviour directed towards another, and the second the behaviour of a person towards whom a behaver role is directed. Thus in a specific marriage there are two behaver roles and two target roles which are closely related but discriminable and taken together form a role set. Concepts like these are potentially able to help grapple with the subtle interplay in marriage between the intrapsychic and the interpsychic, perhaps avoiding some of the conflicts which appear so often when phenomena which are apparently the same are described in competing terms.

Role concepts have a further importance which is that they can deal with longtitudinal as well as situational patterns of responsive behaviour in a way that few other frameworks can offer. For instance, some aspects of a particular behaver role on the part of a wife can be seen as both part of an individual wife role and also the target wife role in response to her husband. The individual wife role is a likely composite with a long historical sequence to which we shall turn later on in this chapter and the target wife role depends on immediate contextual variables. This framework needs detailed clinical studies for elucidation on the scale that Dicks (1967) has given us. However a further problem with his descriptions is not the finely detailed observation but that the explanations which he offers are essentially intrapsychic. Another aspect which we have to consider is that once the marital partner has become 'depressed' and especially if they consult a health professional, they then have the additional possibility of behaving in accordance with the aggregate sick role (Mechanic, 1968). But before the analysis becomes any more complex it is important to understand the developmental sequence which lies behind the marital role set.

### The Genesis of Marital Roles

The creation of the individual marital role far predates the actual decision to marry and in Western societies (like most others for that matter) children begin early to literally 'role-play' the marital roles which they may one day assume. But this, too, is preceded by the more fundamental process of gender ascription and gender indentity. Of these two processes gender identity is the more complex one and defined by Money and Erhardt (1972) as 'the sameness, unity, and persistence of one's individuality as male, female or ambivalent' the public expression of which they call gender role. Although there are undoubted cases of multi-gender biology they are very rare and need not concern us here. Early ascription of gender is the rule, and is one of the very first human responses to a new-born infant. The triumphant cry of 'it's a girl' as the child is born is the first statemant which needs to be made. Statements about the infant's health and integrity soon follow but generally after that first all-important recognition.

From this moment onwards, the differentiation between gender ascription and identity is an active dynamic process between parents and child. Generally the two are consonant but for some new-born children this is not the case and the parents insist on discrepant ascription and identity. Common parental distortions are the firm expectation that the child will be one particular sex rather than the other which in extreme cases is expressed by the parent denying the child's gender. This presents even the relatively young child with the major burden of marked conflict as his or her interpersonal experience away from parents affirms the opposite. A pale version of this struggle is the adopted child's conflict over his 'real' parents and his adoptive ones which is often expressed at adolescence. The issue is the same basic one of the struggle on the child's part to come to terms with deeply-held emotional ideas which are simply not confirmed by everyday experience.

The task for the growing child and parents, 'then, is to develop the appropriate individual and aggregate role which will be the psychological foundation for the later differentiated marital roles. The best possible environment for this is the intact family with both father and mother present (or other adults acting in loco parentis), and also with siblings preferably of both opposite and same sex. Sibling constellation can play an important part in the genesis of gender behaviour as, for example, Brim (1958) has shown, and in the absence of firm gender roles displayed by both parents, good sibling relationships can assume critical importance for the growing child. This is clarified greatly by the careful work which has been done with primates in teasing out the 'familial' influences on the young animals for determining appropriate heterosexual behaviour in adult life. This is well illustrated in the work of Harlow (1962) and his colleagues, and although one can only use these observations as analogues of human behaviour they underline very clearly the importance of this early gender role learning.

This line of argument already makes it clear that it is the reciprocity of behaviour which begins to build up the repertoire of responses which create the perceived picture of gender. This of course includes not only the perception by others of the gender of the child, but also his own perception of himself. In the language of role theory therefore this implies growing integration and increasing differentiation in both the behaver and target roles. This whole process may of course fail, but we shall not be greatly concerned with these kind of failures here since our subject matter assumes that there is at least a minimum of gender differentiation upon which the child can base later marital role behaviour — however inadequate. Between 1 and 3% of any cohort have either an incomplete or a reverse gender role development which then generally prevents them from developing the more complex marital gender role. This appears to be a particular problem amongst people in Western societies and could well be a function of the fairly strong prohibitions on sexual and related behaviour amongst young people. There is plenty of evidence that other more integrated and coherent societies allow their youngsters to experiment with both sexual and marital behaver and target roles from an early age — and suggestions from experimental work with primates are that this facilitates the sexual role behaviour particularly at maturity (see Money and Ehrhardt (1972) for an extended discussion of these issues).

It would be good at this point to be able to refer the reader to definitive studies in which the developmental role history of individuals has been traced with especial emphasis on their subsequent marital performance of these roles. Such evidence is just not available at present — neither for the subsequently disturbed nor for the so-called 'normal'. But there are some retrospective studies which can throw some light on this for us. Of these, some of the most important are those which demonstrate that for people who subsequently suffer from some kind of clinical depressive disorder, a very substantial proportion have also suffered an effective bereavement during their childhood years and, it should be noted, not in their infancy period. Of course this does not appear in the history of all depressed individuals, but its appearance in the history of disordered individuals highlights the role which the intact and present parents must play in the life of the young child. Another most interesting observation which emerges from these studies is that the sex of the parent and the age of the child at the time of the bereavement differ in importance between girls and boys, so that different psychological factors are presumably at play in each sex. But prior to disorder becoming evident, success in marital roles is certainly differentially affected by loss or bereavement. It seems to be more important for potential husbands to have a competent role model than for wives, in the sense that the complementarity of roles seems more contingent on the behaviour of the men than the women. We shall come back to this later in the chapter, but an example of the effect of loss will make the point clearer straight away.

A young man, John, was the eldest child in a marriage which, having produced two children, became increasingly stormy and disturbed. The storms and disturbances were largely apparent in the behaviour of John's mother as she wrestled with the severe emotional problems between herself and her husband. Eventually, and after a series of increasingly bitter outbursts, John's mother left the home when John was about 15, leaving John and his younger sister with their father. John's response to his mother's behaviour was to declare her a 'non-person' and he refused to allow his sister to describe his mother as 'our' mother in his presence. Over the next two years John made several intense relationships with girls about his own age which always ended in the same way when John would become increasingly demanding of their exclusive attention to such an extent that each girl did the sensible thing and left him. Following these episodes John would be most depressed — but fortunately gained increasing understanding of the demanding and unrealistic nature of his construction of the relationship with the young women. Fortunately the story has a happy interim ending. Just before John was 20, his mother became acutely ill and was hospitalized for surgery. At this time, she particularly asked for John to visit her. She had tried to see John in the preceding years but without success. Because she was very ill (and probably because of John's increasing maturity), John agreed to see his mother. At the hospital, what began as a difficult situation, soon developed into a very emotional reconciliation — or more accurately a re-cognition on John's part — which augurs well for the future. John of course was fortunate inasmuch as he had the opportunity to reverse some of the bereavement which he had decided to suffer earlier, but it will remain to be seen what the long-term effect will be upon his subsequent marital role behaviour.

John's experience illustrates the importance of the target role in any role set. Thus, we may assume that John's own gender role was well defined and articulate with other personal behaviour, but the rejecting target role behaviour of his mother was still of great importance so that his gender role behaviour with respect to girls became quite disturbed — with disastrous results (for him) in *their* target role behaviour. The situation is made more complex of course by the fact that John's father is continuing to act as a role-model for him, and we would need to take into account the effect of the father's role behaviour vis-à-vis John's mother to have a complete account. It could well be that the marked change in John's behaviour towards his mother at the time of her illness was due to the fact that his father did not occupy a mediating role in that particular setting, and so had less influence on John's behaviour.

But perhaps this is going too fast and the description of the role set is becoming overly complicated. To return to the simpler formulation, this vignette suggests that the effective loss of one or both parents will have profound effects upon the developing youngster's role development, one part of which is the disabling response of becoming depressed, and that therefore the stage is set for these phenomena to become linked together in complex ways. John's story also highlights the fact that from the beginning, gender role behaviour is inextricably linked with sexual behaviour in the narrow sense and sexuality in the broader sense. Some writers have argued that sex and sexuality are discriminable, which they clearly are in terms of sexual intercourse, since behaviour there is generally much more limited in it's display than other sexually-oriented role behaviour. In fact it is often the case that a man and woman can have a very successful and reciprocal relationship in one of these areas and a disastrous relationship in the other, so that success or failure in the conjugal bed does not by any means always accompany a similar state in the wider sphere of sexuality.

Although this potential for later differentiation is apparent, the child's learning of behaviour in both areas undoubtedly occurs in the same setting and often at the same time. For instance, in controlling, say, masturbatory play, many parents will use the injunction that 'nice little *boys* (not children) don't behave like that' which effectively relates gender and sex role together. From this discussion the reader will have perceived that we are reserving the term gender role for all behaviour offered to another which is gender appropriate, and the more limited terms to specify two aspects of the same behaviour. Generally in Western culture, the growing child is allowed to observe and to exercise much more sexual *role* behaviour than he is straight sexual behaviour. Indeed his chief source of information about adult sexual behaviour may be restricted entirely to films or television — a factor which is often overlooked in our expectation of later competent sexuality. It may well be that discrepancies between these two levels of personal expressiveness are a major contributing factor to subsequent depressive interpersonal experiences but there is no evidence other than clinical to support this possibility at the present time.

## Psychopathology and Role Behaviour

What we have said so far is that even to achieve marriage assumes a modestly successful gender role which has been developed in the context of adequate role models, and that this may be halted or distorted (or both) by psychological trauma which occur in the growing child's interpersonal experience. Thus it seems that although the young person may become potentially capable of entering into an intense dyadic relationship, stresses within early relationships may lead to a pathological response. Perhaps, therefore, before we continue we should examine the intrapsychic explanations of depression to see whether these would fit with the kind of developmental picture we are painting.

Cameron (1963) has given an extended description of the 'depressive' whom he characterises as gloomy and self depreciating leading to pre-occupation with complaints of failure, hopelessness and unworthiness. He says that this behaviour calls forth a response from others which the person finds of no avail to him. Cameron then says this renders the spouse or other person 'impotent' — which confirms the sufferers view of himself. Cameron actually goes on to suggest a developmental framework for the formation of this response which is in essentially interpersonal terms even though his description of the sufferers problems is couched in individual phenomenological terms. As he sees it, the psychological antecedents of depression follow the individual's developmental capacity for making object relations (that is the fundamental ability to relate to another human being). This capacity is related to an infantile helpless dependence which invokes a consequent hostile response from significant people in his environment. This received hostility can then be transposed defensively into the feeling of self-blame which we have noted above. Thus in later life the depression-prone individual can make effective relationships and if problems arise he can sustain these relationships, because the interpersonal conflict about hostile-dependent interactions has already been internalized. It looks, then, as if the interpersonal context is necessary for the subsequent appearance of the depressive response which is the person's adaptation to adverse psychosocial circumstances. This view is one which is strongly supported by Davis (1970) in his adaptational approach to understanding depressive phenomena.

Cameron lists the adverse circumstances as: loss of love and/or emotional support (real or imagined); personal failure — that is failure as perceived by the person; and the threat of new and unknown responsibilities requiring a different or higher level of responsibility. This all implies a vulnerability to the threat of others which may be out of all proportion to the actual threat experienced, so that we shall look in vain for overt early experiences of very hostile threatening parents, who may or may not have been present. Cameron finally notes that the depressed person has expectations for the behaviour of others as well as responding to his own internal world. He expects others to desert him, to rebuff him and belittle him although this is exactly what he does *not* want — rather the reverse. It is the nature of this complex double view which we believe may well set in train the continued 'depressed' behaviour on the part of the disturbed member of the marital partnership.

This formulation is heavily interpersonal in both the suggested aetiology and also in the actual disturbed behaviour. Yet it has long been seen by many writers simply as a disturbance of affect — that is as if something has upset the emotional balance. This clearly completely ignores the characteristic themes and personal constructs, simply treating them as if they were mere epiphenomena of the unbalanced affect. In fact, the two dimensions which run through the account we have offered are those of power, and of emotional expressiveness both of which are also crucial to descriptions of marital roles. What we can say so far is that this psychopathological view does not invalidate the conceptual importance of the gender and marital role conceptions. The role conception is actually further strengthened by examining the clinician's *response* to the depressed patient. In Chapters 5 and 6 the treatment situation is discussed in great detail, but this is an appropriate point to bring out the essentially interpersonal approach by the clinician. Much of the judgement of the patient's level of disturbance is based on the effect on the clinician of the client's behaviour. The clinician often thinks that this is based on direct observation but clearly it is the report of one person to the other about himself which is the vital diagnostic ingredient — and which is of course a role set *par excellence*. There are also independent aspects of the patient's behaviour which the clinician observes such as gait and posture, but diagnostic judgement most often rests on the way in which the patient behaves towards the examiner.

To return to the world of the patient, if the interpersonal world is that important, then is there any evidence to support this idea? There are some retrospective studies of hospitalized patients which give general support to this theme. Cadoret and his colleagues (1972) and Schless and colleagues (1974) have both reported that not only do interpersonal events related to a spouse feature quite disproportionately in the preceding period before clinical depression, but also that these patients feel themselves to be especially vulnerable to marriage-related stresses, and that further, this vulnerability did not disappear when the patient had recovered. This raises the whole question of the antecedent event in the onset of a depressive state, and the evidence of the very thorough study by Brown, Harris and Peto (1973) is convincing that these events are important.

But these workers go further and say that the distinctive feature of the majority of these antecedent events is that of threatened or actual major losses. These they define as separation, or threat of separation from a key figure; new revelations causing a major negative reassessment of a key person; life-threatening illness to such a person; major material loss such as forced rehousing; and finally loss of work. What this study does not do is to specify how a given event is actually handled by the couple which is our emphasis in this account. So we now need to explore the ways in which the individual depressive response as we have outlined it above may be critically brought into play by the way in which marital roles articulate together. This requires us to take a close look at the way in which breakdown in the role-set can occur.

## Normal Marital Role Patterns

For this kind of information the evidence must come partly from successful role-sets in marriage. This has been a constant interest to research workers, but only recently has there been a formulation which gives purchase to the question of the depressive response within marriage. This is the view of marriage as a social system which requires a certain kind of initial structure and a continuous input to the system which not only sustains it but also remains appropriate to the emergent needs of the system. Barry (1970) in his excellent review has assembled much of the evidence now available. He is especially concerned with the importance of prior role models on the genesis of gender and marital role. He takes this into the marital situation by considering the evidence on the continuing perception by one spouse of the other in terms of role behaviour. He summarizes the situation as follows:

'A pattern seems to be emerging from these data. Factors pertaining to the husband appear to be crucial to marital success. Background factors generally considered to lead to a stable male identity, such as happiness of the husband's parents' marriage and the husband's close attachment to his father are related to happiness in marriage. The higher the husband's socioeconomic status and educational level, the greater the marital happiness. The more stable and non-neurotic the husband portrays himself on personality inventories at the time of marriage, the happier the marriage. The higher the wife rates him on emotional maturity as well as on fulfilling his role as husband in conformity to cultural expectations, the happier the marriage. The more the wife comes to resemble her husband on attitude and personality inventories over time, the happier the marriage. It would appear — to generalise a bit — that a solid male identification, established through affectional ties with the father and buttressed by ... the esteem of his wife, is strongly related to happiness in marriage for the couple.'

Barry goes on to develop the line of reasoning that within marriage, women have more difficulty in establishing their overall role, and the quote makes it clear that this is largely because of the much greater dependency which they have upon certain aspects of their husband's role. Their husbands' stability therefore acts as a coherent context for this developmental work to occur — and obviously acts at the same time to underscore the husband's behaver role so that the role set is a reciprocally fulfilling one. Scanzoni (1970) has given substantial confirmation for much of this view in a major study of nearly a thousand couples most carefully selected to be properly representative of the metropolitan area in which the research was carried out. His emphasis is on the key importance of the actual occupational status of husbands in relating the marriage to what he calls the 'opportunity structure' of the society but, in addition, the evidence he cites for reciprocal role performance as being quite critical is most impressive. At this point a note of caution should be sounded. Most of this research has been carried out in the USA and therefore might be seen as inapplicable to other Western industrial countries. Yet although this caveat is important, the major role expectations are derived from common cultural sources and it seems highly likely that the broad pattern is applicable outside the USA.

In one sense these studies and others like them appear to give support to Parsons and Bales (1955) much-criticized description of the aggregate role prescriptions for husbands and wives. This famous discrimination was between the 'expressive' roles of wives and the 'instrumental' roles of husbands which was said to operate particularly towards the children in the family. Our concern here is obviously with the marital relationship rather than the parent–child relationship and it may be important to discriminate between them when we consider the truth of Parson's differentiation. There is certainly plenty of evidence from all sides to suggest that the role differences between mothers and fathers are now much less marked than they used to be, but evidence for a change between the married partners is not nearly as clear. Indeed, the evidence which Barry has summarized, and Scanzoni's work (both of which are firmly rooted in empirical study) suggest that role behaviour between normal spouses is still differentiated along these dimensions. The important emphasis is, however, on reciprocity of behaviour rather than on aggregate role structure. It may well be that changes in the whole basis of these relationships is imminent, but for the moment this cannot be a statement of fact. At the level of task role differences, Crawford (1972) found in her study that the patterns were fairly sharply differentiated in a middle-aged sample. But reciprocity is very important, and extreme segregation of role behaviour may well accompany individual psychological disturbance. Certainly this was the case with the marriages of neurotic men which Collins and co-workers (1971) studied where they found that role differentiation was much more marked than in a normal non-neurotic sample.

Differentiating between marital roles in this way may seem actually old-fashioned in the present climate when the question of marriage as a complete partnership is very much to the fore. The notion that in the marital pair the role of husband may be the cardinal one may appear to suggest that the role of wife is a subordinate one. This is not the case. It is possible that the view which we are developing here of the successful role structure may need modifying when the evidence accrues, but this role structure does *not* imply weakness or passivity on the part of a wife. In fact, the situation is quite the reverse since if a husband's roles at work and at home are both well-founded, then the implication is that the wife's roles can be more clearly (and more rewardingly) developed. Because the couple set up a psychological system, then the husbands development of his role is aided by the success of his wife.

What is vitally important is to recognize that we are discussing the dynamic marital relationship and not the static one. Thus we should expect change to occur during the course of the relationship because it is the actual role structures which interest us, and not the more formal aggregate roles which are seen as part of the general social structure. These developmental changes in role which may be of great importance in understanding depression are discussed in later chapters.

If the aggregate role structure in the culture did change markedly then the picture would have to be redrawn, but this would require radical and profound changes in the basic concepts of gender identity and role and there is little evidence that this is happening. The strident statements of radical women's groups might suggest otherwise but adequate research like that of Young and Willmott (1973) does not support them. What they do suggest is that domestic arrangements have changed and will continue to change, but that the role patterns which are probably important in the psychopathology of marriage work at a more profound level. Concepts like the 'companionate marriage' and the 'symmetrical family' may alter the balance rather than alter the deep structure.

## Inadequate Marital Roles and Depression

From these lines of work we now have two suggestions for the breakdown of marital roles which we can use. The work we have been discussing suggests that inadequate, and possibly pathological role relationships develop when a husband has an insecure gender role, and also inadequate or conflictual models for the behaver role of husband in its many aspects. Further, that the effective creation of satisfactory marital roles is even less likely to occur if the husband is poorly placed with respect to the 'economic opportunity structure'.

Taken singly or together, these factors then make the other spouse's efforts to organize her role in response to her husband's uncertainties very difficult. It is even possible that the pair are originally drawn together because they sense similar difficulties in each other which gives them a feeling of understanding. But the depressive response may be already pre-potent in the sense that neither partner has achieved a proper sense of his or her own mastery in the situation and thus either one or both are very vulnerable to actual or threatened loss. Because this account is dealing with adults, the emphasis is on the interactional effects of the mature individuals rather than their earlier developmental history. This does not deny the importance of the historical factors as we have already discussed earlier in this chapter, but it places special emphasis on the unique way in which these work out in the marital roles. In the general situation we are describing here, the capacity to cope with conflict may be quite limited because of the threatening nature of such behaviour to the depression-prone spouse. So denial is used as a mutually defensive manoeuvre. But ultimately some situation arises which intensely stimulates the inadequate feelings of one spouse who responds to this with depression. If the other spouses response to this is ineffectual then new roles may appear based on the 'depressive premise' which may then only be redefined more healthily again with expert help.

Yet none of this problem may be at all obvious to the casual observer. We have perhaps apparently painted the picture of two incompetent or ineffective people trying unsuccessfully to support each other in threatening situations. In fact the individuals concerned are often very competent in certain spheres of activity which may only be affected when the depressive system is well under way. Indeed, it is often the case that it is this very awareness of former competence which often leads to an intensification of the depressive difficulty initially. This is often what is so baffling and perplexing to the spouse, since he/she may only see the potential competence and not the actual deep doubt and despair.

A recent large-scale statistical study of clinical patients underscores this type of analysis which we are offering. In this work Overall (1971) was interested in the relation between symptom patterns and marital status. He studied the records of 2,000 patients retrospectively and found that 'depressive mood' and 'guilt' were much more likely to occur amongst the married and also the once-divorced than amongst the other social statuses. The other groups were much more likely to have other kinds of symptomatic responses such as anxiety. These are statistical relationships which result from a multiple discriminant analysis of the data, but Overall goes on to suggest that they are important and psychologically significant. In discussing the results he writes:

'The prominence of depressive symptoms in married and once-married groups requires special consideration ... it is conjectured that the phenomena have to do with dependency relationships in a less than adequate social situation.'

It is the set of 'dependency relations' as he puts it which may then set the scene for the later disturbance. These are centrally concerned with the emotional needs of each partner, and in particular the capacity of either to meet the demands of the other, without the vicious circle of intropunitive responses starting up. The relationship pattern is therefore likely to be different in the case of the marriage which starts off as being a 'pathology protector' than that in which later role changes disturb the fragile equilibrium and subsequently bring about the pathological pattern. Two examples from our clinical experience will make the point of these differences much clearer. The first describes the marriage apparently created to solve a role problem.

Mr. and Mrs. X had been married about three years when Mrs. X became very depressed and became a psychiatric in-patient. They were a working class couple, with one small child aged six months, living quite near both their parental homes. Mr. X was a 'good' husband who did everything he could to help his wife and to keep the home running effectively. As she became progressively more disabled so Mr. X took over more of her role but with very little ability to really meet her emotional needs — or even to understand them. Investigation of this couple's marriage revealed that Mrs. X had a capable mother who never allowed her the chance to experiment with failure. She cast her husband into a similar role which he all-too-fully accepted. However, their role relationship was really very different since he did not provide the covert emotional support which her mother had always done. Therefore her feelings of inadequacy and her resentment against the source of this feeling (her husband), were enhanced to the point at which the defensive properties of the marriage proved quite inadequate and her husband's caring style increased rather than decreased their problems. This couple obviously had a collusive agreement that Mrs. X's dependent role with her mother would be identical to that with her husband. Even so this took no account of her actual change in status when she had her own child. He was unable to give her the support which she needed to become an autonomous wife because of the way in which the role expectations had been set up. In early marriage this precarious marital system survived but then when she became a mother herself the old conflicts came to the fore. Her husband intensified his behaviour — perhaps in order to protect her — but the conflict was so intense that she became demoralized and depressed. In fact, this response was actually the key to a very productive and maturing change which the couple undertook in the therapeutic setting and which radically altered the marital role-set.

The second example illustrates the pathological response to a role set which has worked quite effectively but then comes to grief because of its inherent inflexibility to meet a different set of emotional needs. We have envisaged a given role-set in marriage as acting to keep the internal feelings of guilt and worthlessness at bay. The problem with such an ultra-stable system is that no change can be envisaged because this immediately stimulates the depressive reaction. But outside events are often uncontrollable and bring about just this undesirable change for which the marital pair now has no coping mechanism. Mr. and Mrs. Y had been married about 23 years. For much of this time they had lived abroad as successful senior executive and family much involved in both commercial and social events in very responsible ways. Following his retirement back to England the family had initially settled well, especially Mrs. Y, who rapidly became involved in a quite different lifestyle from the one which she had experienced overseas, and which gave her a good deal more autonomy. Her husband, however, did not prosper and despite various enterprises became increasingly withdrawn and gloomy. His wife was most concerned with his response but could not apparently find any way by which his increasing sense of failure could be diminished. Investigation of this couple (who were treated on an outpatient basis) soon revealed that their roles had essentially been a very stylized version of the middle-class aggregate role to which they had been exposed when they were young. During their time abroad their well-practised and largely autonomous marital roles had been supported by the context in which they lived and no problems appeared despite Mr. Y's personal feeling of some inadequacy. The return home threatened the whole structure but they had no interpersonal techniques which which to handle the tensions. Mrs. Y's attempt to remedy things only increased Mr. Y's sense of inadequacy and also his incapacity to communicate to her his real emotional needs. As the therapy proceeded Mr. Y tried even more desperately to create a useful new work role for himself but without success. And of course each failure increased his sense of worthlessness. This occurred also despite the effort of the therapist to help him see what he was doing. Change came when he stopped trying to conform to some non-existent aggregate role within his culture and began to work out what *he* wanted to do — probably for the first time in his life. This then enabled him to work with the new role which his wife had already begun to adopt but which up to that point had been disabling rather than enabling for him.

The important difference between these two cases is the way in which the initial marital role set was created. In the first instance the marriage as a pathology protector soon crumbled leaving the couple with virtually no emotional resources to sustain their lives together — and in fact the young wife made several suicide attempts. The older couple, on the other hand, had the advantage of at least their well-practised habitual style which did enable them to move towards a more rewarding response pattern and subsequently role-set. Their problem was much more related to loss of an external identifying role and a reversal of the dependency pattern.

These two examples also illustrate another important point about the marital roles in depressed couples. In neither case would one describe the marriage as poor — meaning relationships which were characterised by overt conflict, poor superficial communication, or immaturely selfish behaviour. Rather they both appeared superficially to be adequate and supportive so that to the outsider the onset of depression in one partner appears to be quite baffling. Indeed as the process continues the depressed partner may take upon him/herself the blame for both his own problems and those of the other members of the family. So much so, that the non-disturbed spouse may be quite prevented from feeling even a reasonable amount of guilt in the situation. Even justifiable anger on the part of the non-depressed spouse can be internalized by the depressed partner as further proof of their baleful effect on their partner.

Beneath this there is often another, and a more disturbed, level of experience which is quite negatively and aggressively toned and which may break through. This often appears to have been a long-standing characteristic of the role set but one which has never been acknowledged. It is at this level that the marriage may have been poor in just the ways which our two cases illustrate, so that they have a brittleness which often superficially appears as strength.

## The Sick Role

At some stage in some depressive disturbances, the disturbed partner or his spouse decide to call in outside help to intervene in the process. Whoever the consultant is, the act of calling in someone outside the family means that another role-set has been brought into play which will affect the existing structure. In a later chapter there will be much more detailed discussion of the therapeutic problems which arise from this process, but here we want to focus down on the importance of the particular role-set arising in health care situations. This is widely known as the sick role. The sick role has been studied in a number of pathologies, but not especially in depressive disorders and so the discussion must necessarily be based on a general understanding of the issues involved.

By the time the person consults, say, a physician, the marital pattern surrounding the depressed spouse has already become fairly stable. But the act of consulting will obviously affect this stability in a number of ways. If the spouse has decided that he/she is 'ill' and the other spouse agrees, then provided that the doctor responds in like manner the marital set is already prepared for the impact of the sick role. The most important single change which this construction can bring about that responsibility for treatment now falls squarely on to the physician, and the spouses no longer have to wrestle with the interpersonal problems which the disturbance has brought. The most troublesome area in the depressed situation is often that of ambivalent dependence and this aspect of the disturbed spouse's behaviour may simply shift over completely to the health professional. Paradoxically this may be quite crucial to enable the marital roles to be re-aligned in order to function more effectively. The partner is relieved of the problems of having to respond to the dependent demands of the patient and can then afford to be much more forthcoming in his caring behaviour since the task now is mutual cooperation with the doctor.

If the process of consultation follows the path we have outlined then the two role-sets are smoothly related together and the sick role can be accommodated to the marital roles. But the sick role set is hopefully a transitional one which patient and professional occupy briefly, and the work of re-alignment in the marital roles has to go on during this period. For the vast majority of disorders this is indeed the case so that by the end of the 'treatment' period not only can the patient relinquish the sick role but also the viability of the patient as a marital partner is restored.

Less effective resolution of the sick role-set is also possible. Problems arise when the patient relinquishes the role of spouse and embraces the patient role in its entirety. Thus the two role-sets are not kept congruent with each other and there is a steady loss of marital role behaviour. This then only exacerbates the deprecatory thinking of the patient so that he/she becomes increasingly passive-dependent. Hospitalization may enhance such a process unless great care is exercised — a problem of real proportions to the health professionals involved. Fortunately many modern hospital environments discourage these processes and especially with the depressed person. The importance of maintaining the marital role set is therefore most important in the light of the possible benefits and damage which may result from the sick role. The difficulties largely turn on the question of individual responsibility for struggling with the problems. This may well be redistributed between the people involved at various times in the handling of the disorder, but the ultimate aim is obviously to restore a proper balance in the marital role structure so that responsibility is restored and the depressive pattern is no longer required.

**Some Conclusions**

This has been a necessarily complicated chapter. Both here and in the preceding chapter we have tried to bring together concepts and ideas which have not generally been associated with each other. The emphasis is of course on interpersonal models of disturbance, but in the discussion we have tried to show that this model can encompass the earlier models based on intrapsychic function alone. We have also made things more complicated for ourselves by including the notion that the role-set which includes the 'sick role' is often an important part of the solution to the depression. It is just too easy to see this as a rather alien intervention from outside the marital system, when in fact it has the most direct effects on the system itself, both for good and ill.

The personal historical factors in setting up marital role patterns are obviously important and we have spelled these out in some detail. In the section devoted to this, we emphasized the importance of gender role, and recent work has underlined this view. At the moment the evidence of the importance of gender role in the development of depression in marriage is largely confined to women. It is now a well-established fact that about twice as many women as men become clinically depressed in all of the Western countries which have undertaken competent research. Until very recently this difference was generally accounted for by referring to the differing hormonal biochemistry of the two sexes, and especially the fact that in both child-birth and in the menopause there may well be considerable instability. However, a very careful recent review by Weissman and Paykel (1977) finds little evidence for these explanations or even for increased levels of depression at times of hormonal imbalance except during the post-natal period.

They prefer psychosocial explanations if only because these can also account for the increased rate of depressive disorders in younger women over the last thirty years, and dismiss the idea that this incidence is a product of the way in which women use health services or are especially aware of emotional problems. They say:

'The most convincing evidence that social role plays an important part in the vulnerability of women to depression is the data that suggest that marriage has a protective effect for males but a detrimental effect for women ... Further understanding of social stress and its interaction with components of the female vulnerability in the traditional role is a promising area of research. This research would need to take into account intervening variables such as womens' employment and the quality of the marriage.'

The great pity is that so far the psychosocial position of depressed men has not been subject to the same amount of enquiry. We have suggested in this chapter that similar factors may be at work although in dissimilar ways, and even though it is obviously right to focus attention on the much larger number of depressed women, the absolute number of depressed men is itself high. Certainly it is increasingly clear that our understanding of depression can only increase as we study the contemporary marital role sets in which depressed husbands and wives find themselves.

# 3

# PREDISPOSING AND STRESSFUL EVENTS IN MARRIAGE

In this chapter we will build on the interactive concepts already described, and use them to examine the dynamics and adaptive processes of the married couple in dealing with the demands of life events and critical life stages in their relationship. We will incorporate and integrate into our ideas the body of information and data of other workers in the field, in their analysis of the differential influence of multiple stresses and interpersonal difficulties in precipitating depression.

Our first consideration must be for the interactive event of marriage itself and the ensuing expectations that it subsumes for a whole new range of different patterns of behaviour in the individuals concerned. Each individual has to acknowledge the change of status that it confers in relation to the family group, the wider social network as well as the new role that society imposes on the married individual. Agreeing to pass through the ritual of the marriage ceremony implies an overt declaration of a willingness or a readiness to undergo this change of status and responsibility. From here on there is a continued demand for an awareness and sensitivity to another person's behaviour and emotional needs and this includes the awareness of learning to display care and concern within the framework of a loving relationship. This life transition provides an opportunity for a weakening of the bonds between the individual and his/her family of origin and for a step forward or a maturational gain through a new relationship with different definitions and objectives. Hence there is a weening away from the old emotional ties and a questing for new resources and strengths within the intimacy of a yet untested relationship. If this transition is to occur successfully there must be trust, affection and commitment to the changing role and the two partners must create the conditions wherein they can make their individual needs explicit. They also have to learn to negotiate ways of meeting each other's demands without making such major personal sacrifices as to prejudice later transactions between them. Fletcher (1966) writes of contemporary marriage 'that the successful working out of relationships and problems depends more and more upon continual individual effort' and 'it calls for a great degree of personal adjustment and for continual care and mutual consideration'. Similarly Dicks (1967) describes the psychoanalytic model for a complete marriage as 'the full and undisturbed flow of two way communication between the conscious and unconscious parts of two people in flexible role changes, with each partner able to identify with and tolerate the regressive or infantile needs of the other when occasion demands'.

In the early stages of marriage there is usually an initial cautiousness or holding back, and an extra tolerance for misunderstandings and irritations. This imposes a degree of rigidity and artificiality which cannot last and the small resentments grow into major feelings of hostility and ill-concealed aggression. The couple's first row develops and they have the opportunity to express freely their feelings about each other and as a result of this confrontation can formulate rules to negotiate their future differences. These rules (Haley, 1963) are not made explicit, but by mutual agreement at a verbal and also at a non-verbal or implicit level, they become understood as guidelines for future confrontations. Through each transaction individual couples evolve an idiosyncratic style for themselves and resort to this pattern in future negotiations. Failures at this stage of the developing relationship can lead to unsatisfactory rule making for one or both partners with associated misconceptions and misunderstandings and a gradual breakdown of trust and honesty between partners.

Haley saw these rules emerging as constraints or regulators within the marital system. Homeostasis is preserved as a result of circular and not linear interactive processes occuring between individuals and the direction and intensity of the process is controlled or modified by the emergence of rules which re-establish a new level of adjustment or equilibrium. We want to argue that depressive behaviour can be construed as one of these regulators and become the emergent quality of the interpersonal system. Coyne (1976) argues along these same lines that the depressed person and members of his social environment become enmeshed in a system where genuine feedback cannot be received and further that efforts to change only become system maintaining. The depressed person is confronted by a series of interactive stalemates which he can only resolve either by losing support and validation by others or by displaying more symptoms.

Other writers such as McPartland and Hornstra (1964) and Klerman (1974) have studied the communicative value of depressive behaviour and seen it as serving a potentially adaptive function which at a later stage becomes maladaptive and therefore equivalent to Coyne's concept of 'interactive stalemates'. Klerman argues that depressive behaviour 'initiates a hyperexic response (one which disturbs the organisms homeostasis) and produces a negative feedback pattern which further alienates the patient from social supports, impairing his effectiveness and his instrumental and affective roles and hindering his biological homeostasis.'

We are suggesting therefore that depressive behaviour becomes the end result of a series of interactive blunders and misunderstandings where the resources of the interpersonal system can no longer deal with the pressure of new emotional demands and role changes. Thus once the system has made its new adjustment and depressive behaviour emerges as a 'signal' (Klerman) of the quality of the underlying relationships, additional problems arise in shifting the system back to its non-depressive equilibrium. The individuals have taken up new positions vis-á-vis each other which are dependent on a continuity of the depressive behaviour in one partner. In other words their ongoing behaviour fosters the continued emergence of the depressive symptoms. The depressive woman's behaviour may become a reason for her partner to withdraw emotionally from her. His own sense of guilt at his personal failure to deal with her demands drives him into either an artificial position of restrained patience and long continued reassurances, or a more overt rejection pattern of personal avoidance where he hands over to a medical authority and opts out of the responsibilities himself.

But our task is to clarify the factors which disturb the homeostasis of the system and thereby give rise to the interactive problems we have described.

The system has a limited capacity to absorb and deal with stresses and strains and this is determined by the level to which the couple's patterns of behaviour are governed by their own sets of 'rules'. If rules are rigidly defined and adhered to and the next level of meta rules or 'rules about rules' is equally strict then the couple offer themselves little latitude for variations in their repertoire in relation to each other. In this situation the system will be a vulnerable one and will be subjected to greater stress much sooner.

If rules about relationships are to be effective, they must be subjected to continual reassessment and redefinition in order to deal with changing needs within the relationship. The more flexible the system is then the better it is able to absorb and deal with change.

At this point we will move away from our theoretical framework and take a more practical look at some of the problems inherent in the intimate bond of marriage. The work of Sullivan (1953) sharpens our understanding of the drives and motivations that bring two people together in a relationship. He proposed that the great need of the developing individual was to reduce anxiety by seeking security and satisfaction. To achieve this goal individuals came together to gratify their primary needs and the length of their association was entirely determined by their ability to sustain these satisfactions. 'The goal of a person who is integrated with another may be said to be the achievement of satisfaction under conditions in which security is maintained or enhanced.' He also notes in interactive terms that if one individual is unable to seek his needs for satisfaction and security in the relationship then his behaviour makes it impossible for the other to enjoy a full experience. He describes malevolently transformed behaviour where the child learns, in his search for tenderness, that his behaviour is only greeted by parental rebuffs and therefore resorts to angry demanding behaviour from his 'bad me' which generates an emotional response in his parents and becomes his only reward and therefore is associated with anxiety. Although his observations do not directly relate to marriage they illustrate needs and patterns of behaviour encountered within the marital relationship.

The search for security and satisfaction within the marriage may render the individual vulnerable and at risk. Lack of satisfactions in previous relationships may have been tolerated with the romantic fantasy that one day the right person would appear and the ideal relationship would then be just round the corner. This presupposes a tremendous emotional investment in the need for rightness and fit within the desired relationship. The partner may be given such an idealized role that any chances for a successful and realistic adaptation are prejudiced from the start.

Hence individual expectations may be sadly misconstrued because they are a projection of the individual's dissatisfactions and insecurities within their childhood relationships. One sees an extreme example of this pattern in the behaviour of the young girl who may be the product of a broken marriage and who leaves her home at the earliest possible age to precipitate herself into intense relationships. She searches hungrily for emotional fulfilment but ends up on a disaster course of illegitimate pregnancies, early marriage, attempted suicides, treatment for depression and marital breakdown.

On the other hand where goals and expectations fit in with reality and both marital partners do have a good capacity for mutual adjustment, trust and intimacy, then the state of marriage can offer support and stability for the individuals and serve a protective function at times of stress.

There is some disagreement in the literature about the protective role of marriage. In a Review article Crago (1972) suggests that those who emphasize environmental factors maintain that marriage has a protective and stabilizing influence on the partners and protects against mental disorder. However, within marriage she notes that the rates of neurosis as well as hospitalization and rehospitalization are higher in wives than husbands. She suggests that wives need to make a bigger adjustment within marriage in order to take on their traditional expressive, integrative and accommodating role and thereby render themselves more vulnerable than their partners. Another female investigator Robertson (1974) supports these views from the results of a study of the marital status of all referrals to psychiatric care in NE Scotland over a set period of time (9,776 cases). She found that amongst the young married women there were higher rates of neurotic depression, character and behaviour disorders than amongst comparable single women. Therefore she proposes that marriage poses an additional strain for the young woman which may lead to mental breakdown.

Porter (1970) emphasized the depression prone vulnerability of married women from a General Practice Survey. This was not age related although he found a social class difference; the wives of aspiring manual workers showed a greater vulnerability than the non-manual workers' wives. Single women were almost entirely spared from depressive illness in his sample. However, Overall (1971) emphasizes the importance of marital history and not simply the social status of marriage as a predetermining factor for assessing manifest psychopathology. He argues from his American study of 2,000 patients that repeated marriages may be related to increasing levels of social effectiveness. Hence he sees the status of marriage as signifying evidence of both social competence and personal acceptability. In this group of patients he suggests that the once married are a group who share relatively high levels of depressive symptomatology and may be considered culturally bound, semi-social individuals where there is a highly developed super-ego which may punish in certain ways yet holds these people together in an unhappy marriage. Those patients with multiple marriages represent a group who are socially more competent, less reticent to seek help and who deal with their problems by overt acting out behaviour. He understands the first marriage to act as a screen for schizoid withdrawal and bizarreness and second marriage as a screen for depressive tendencies. These findings are very thought-provoking in their supposition that divorce and remarriage for vulnerable couples may represent a development from the depressive interaction to a more healthy relationship. But now we should look at some of the precursors of these adult patterns.

## Influences of Early Childhood Relationships

In a discussion of the major sources of strength in a marriage Blood and Wolfe (1960) include the couple's homogamy from the point of view of shared interests and expectations, and the extent to which they meet each other's needs. We would like to consider the homogamy of the background families in terms of their influence on the social patterns of behaviour of their products in the next generation. The growing child has usually only one identity model for his future behaviour in marriage and learns from watching his parents a style of interaction which becomes incorporated as his/her own. Their way of dealing with conflict, intimacy and affection becomes the platform from which the young person experiments with life. The pattern may be to greet conflict with conflict, or conflict with avoidance and conceal open expressions of feeling or limit them to very safe situations. The young person witnesses a recurring cycle of transactions and frequently incorporates his parents' rules for dealing with the situation to such an extent that he involuntarily responds in a similar way when confronted by the self-same problems in his own marriage. When his partner brings a different set of rules and expectations there can be a confusion and misunderstanding of the other's underlying messages and rules. The young person marrying straight from home particularly may have little experience and developed little tolerance for another alien style of living. They may equate parental patterns with safe styles of living and become very perplexed by a different value system which discounts the old well-tried ways. Success in adapting will depend on their individual capacity to be flexible and to change.

Hooper and Sheldon (1969) discuss the problems of the newly married couples in their study and emphasize that couples who head for trouble at this point in their lives are those whose problems arise out of the interactions of the couple themselves and who demonstrate little capacity for empathy or understanding with each other and little capacity for decision making.

We have said already that we understand the act of marriage itself as serving a maturational gain for the individual. It represents another life stage and an opportunity to reduce or sever emotional links with past key figures. However this presupposes a willingness and a capacity to make this move forward and away from previous involvements. In order to do this the individual must already have begun the process of self individuation and differentiation during the adolescent years. If the search for identity has not begun the individual starts from a very immature position. Erikson(1956) describes the importance of identity formation 'in order to fit new experience into it and expand it to meet new experiences before one is able to be intimate with anyone else'. His last phrase is of great importance as it highlights the relevance of emotional separation from old attachments before a total and intimate emotional commitment can be made within a new relationship.

Unresolved oedipal conflicts are common examples of potentially damaging attachments which can set the scene for choice of marital partner. There is a relentless search to gain emotional fulfillment by setting up a parallel relationship within the marriage. However the individual is hampered by neurotic inferiority feelings and an ambivalence towards the desired object and the aggressive and destructive urges which are revived once again prejudice their opportunities for success. This can set the scene for unfulfilled needs and depressive patterns of behaviour.

The importance of seeing oneself as an adequate personality through one's childhood experiences is emphasized by Seligman (1974) who discusses the kind of childhood experience which protect the adult against the debilitating effects of helplessness and depression. He suggests that the child needs experiences in which he sees his own actions as being instrumental in bringing about gratifications and removing annoyances. 'To see oneself as an effective human being may require a childhood filled with powerful synchronies betweening responding and its consequences'. In other words the individual needs to have the experience of childhood success in relationships in order to succeed in adult ones. This is a behavioural observation based on his experience with dogs and may not make sufficient allowance for the learning ability and capacity for change demonstrated by the adult human.

Rapoport (1967) summarizes some of these points and describes the processes of marriage and the critical role transitions as 'tasks'. She delineates three critical subphases which must be worked through by the young couple, namely the engagement period leading to the Rite de-passage, the honeymoon and the early marriage period. At each phase both personal and interpersonal adjustments must be made. In addition she sees three potential issues for intervention and these are (a) intrapsychic problems which preceded the marriage, (b) problems relating to a dominant relationship between one partner and an external figure, (c) problems connected with taking on realistic roles after marriage which may be in the sexual area or may relate to a failure to drop the idealized pre-marriage image of the partner. This latter problem she considers relates more frequently to the wife, who becomes unable to view her husband realistically and precipitates herself into the frustration of an artificial relationship leading eventually to depression and misery.

We will now illustrate some of these key issues in effective early marital adjustment by reference to the case history of a couple who came for help after five years of marriage with longstanding sexual difficulties and depression in the wife. The wife had come from a family where personal needs tended to take second place to the goals of achievement in altruistic activities outside the family group. Her father became a remote unavailable, depression-prone individual and gave little time to his children. As a result she grew up in a busy household feeling lost and neglected, and discovered that she achieved greater recognition when she showed the 'bad side' of her personality (especially where her father was concerned). She saw her parents as rather separate people and feelings of affection were rarely shown. She grew up to believe that one day she would meet the right man who would supply all her needs emotionally and sexually. She began a long and devoted courtship with her husband in her teenage years and had great expectations for the immediate success of her marriage. It soon became clear that her emotional needs were not to be satisfied and her dissatisfactions showed themselves in angry depressive sulking and emotional and sexual avoidance. Her husband became confused and hurt by her behaviour and withdrew into various intellectual pre-occupations; only showed his frustrations occasionally. Because she had created a very rigid value system she displayed considerable difficulty in giving up her hurt misunderstood depressive role during treatment. Her childhood experiences had left her with an idealized view of later marriage and also a great need to find the emotional recognition and fulfillment she had missed in earlier years.

## The Effects of the Early Years of Marriage

The modern scene is producing an extended early marriage period before the birth of the first child. This has been determined by more effective contraceptive techniques and the advent of the 'pill', and also the changing attitude towards the enjoyment of sexual activity for its own sake. Economic pressures for mortgage and a high material standard of living make the wife's continued earnings a necessity. In addition the career conscious wife has the opportunity to plan her family and limit its size as she wishes, leaving her more personal freedom to develop her own special interests and talents. This new pattern offers both advantages and disadvantages. It gives the young couple more time to develop their own relationship and to achieve a greater level of understanding and mutual satisfaction, but it may also mean that they evolve a rigid routine which becomes the safe part of their relationship and which will be very disrupted and altered after the first baby's arrival. For economic reasons then the planned first child is tending to arrive later in the woman's life and after the years which are usually described as the biological ones for reproduction.

The birth of a baby leads to major changes in a wife's style of living. She now finds herself committed totally to the demands of a dependent being and has to orientate much more completely to her domestic role. This of itself isolates her from her previous supports and opportunities for fulfilment of her emotional needs and she is confronted for the most part with the reality of turning to her husband as her total source of support and reassurance. Her own personal resources for adaptation and readjustment are suddenly put to the test. Her capacity to form a warm loving intimate relationship with her baby is exposed and she must learn to deal with any feelings of hostility or rejection when they arise. Once again our modern style of living is not very helpful at this point of stress. As a result of social mobility relatives tend to live at a distance or remain in city centres while the young move out to new estates on the outskirts of large conurbations. Young husbands tend to be very work orientated either because of their own developing careers or because they are attempting to take on overtime in order to assist the family budget. The more resourceful young wives on new estates offer each other a measure of support and help, but the young wife who is running into major problems in relation to her new role and becoming depressed and miserable will isolate herself from others and become involved in an increasing downward spiral, in which her husband finds he cannot offer much help. This may set the scene for puerperal depression.

Two prospective studies (Pitt, 1968; Dalton 1971) have attempted to identify the factors which predispose to puerperal depression and post partum 'blues'. They both found high levels of anxiety during pregnancy to be a feature. Dalton describes labile emotions in 64% of her sample. She finds a link between women who have premenstrual symptoms and puerperal depression and suggest it may represent a difficulty in adjusting to hormone changes. Pitt found a fear of abnormal pregnancy predominated. Lomas (1967) suggests personality characteristics are of key importance and describes the predisposed individual as typically immature, with idealized expectations for the baby, lacking personal flexibility to deal with the variable hazards of the confinement. Breakdown therefore occurs as a result of the combination of her personal rigidity, the temperament of the baby and the vicissitudes of the environmental setting during the puerperium. In his own study he found his patients had an unhappy relationship with their own parents and were lacking in spontaneity and a free expression of their sexuality. Their own personal frigidity leads to difficulties in meeting the babies' emotional demands.

For some families it is the arrival of the second child which produces the major strains and problems. The wife suddenly finds herself totally occupied with the conflicting demands of a new baby and a changed toddler, who is no longer the charming cooperative youngster that she knew befor his sibling arrived, but has become noisy, demanding and interfering as he works out his own feelings of competition and displacement. It is at this stage that the wife tends to become emotionally depleted and irritable and has little energy left to meet her husband's emotional and sexual needs at the end of the day.

The husband for his part has to be prepared to share his wife with the new arrivals and can no longer expect to gain her individual interest and attention. For the selfish immature and dependent male this poses major problems and for some their adaptation may be to dissociate themselves from the family scene, by taking on additional work commitments or by arriving home after the children have been put to bed. Others may take a symmetrical role with their wife and share the new responsibilities. However this is a very critical adjustment and many marriages begin to flounder at this stage, as the wife becomes increasingly hostile and resentful at her partner's lack of concern and responsibility and withdraws emotionally in order to punish him. It is not long before she is labelled anxious, depressed and frigid and the husband becomes confused, disappointed and sexually frustrated. Their mutual capacity for trust and intimacy becomes very strained and they exist side by side feeling increasingly alienated, tense and bitter at the turn of their fortunes.

A recent study (Brown 1975) has focused down on the social and emotional problems of a sample of depressed women living in South London. The findings illustrated two very important factors which contribute to depression: (1) social class. He found a higher rate of disturbance amongst working class wives (25%) than middle class wives (5%). (2) life stage, age, marital status and age of youngest child at home. He found the group of young women with a child under the age of six years, had a particularly high rate of disturbance. However the working class wives were particularly vulnerable (working class 42%, middle class 5%). The reasons for the 'at risk' quality of this particular group of women related to crises involving husband, children and housing. The working class wives had more threats of eviction, more husbands unemployed or in prison and more sons in trouble with the Police for breaking and entering. These differences disappeared when the older age groups were examined.

These findings only accounted for 20% of the variance between groups and he questioned why five times as many working class wives became depressed after a major life event than middle class. In a search for a vulnerability factor he examined the quality of their interpersonal relationships with their partners (male or female) and derived a four point scale ranging from a close intimate relationship to a confidante seen rarely or not at all. He was able to show that high intimacy in interpersonal relationships offered protection against severe life events and that of his working class sample only 4% had a good intimate relationship and 42% had a poor one. The pattern for intimacy over the years of marriage also varied for the two social groups. The middle class marriages showed a slow decline in intimacy values with time whereas the working class showed a sharp drop for intimacy values in the early years of marriage when young children were in the home, and later the levels recovered to middle class levels after the children had left home. The vulnerability factors seem to be crucial to the sense of self-esteem for the young wife who may become depressed through a sense of failure, loss and demoralization. He suggests that they contribute to the lack of confidence and resourcefulness of the working class wife to deal with the stresses of major life events and also that they may be a feature of our present industrial and urbanized society.

In summary then, we have discussed and considered the stresses in interpersonal terms of the early years of marriage and have referred to original research which supports the notion that vulnerability increases particularly for young married women and especially those from a working class background.

## The Middle Years of Marriage

We have spent some time considering the problems of the early years of marriage and will now consider other critical times where there may be sudden changes in patterns of behaviour in an apparently previously stable relationship and where no obvious external life event has occurred to precipitate a depressed pattern of behaviour in one or both partners. Paykel (1971) supports this notion in a study where he observed that amongst 15–20% of a group of depressed women no obvious precipitating event had occurred. It is therefore at the interpersonal level that we must seek for answers to these observations. Life stages, like marriage, are times of critical transition where there is a 'task' to be undertaken in order that the individuals may adapt to the changing needs and roles of their current marital relationship.

One critical period is the time of emancipation from child rearing obligations where the children are first becoming adolescent and then later leaving home (empty nest). It is a time for interpersonal re-alignments within the family system, an acknowledgement of the weakening bonds between parent and children and a new awareness of the importance of husband—wife bonds. It may also be a time when increased demands are being made for emotional support by the aging members of the previous generation and also for the wife the beginnings of her menopause and an appreciation that she is now entering middle age. Gynaecological symptoms associated with changing menstrual patterns may become a feature. The more frequent use of the hysterectomy operation as the best way to deal with the problem often then creates its own difficulties. Anxieties may be generated about the woman's role both sexually and as a wife. Hysterectomies are frequently held to blame for changing sexual performance and lack of sexual enjoyment. However although the quality of sexual response may change and gynaecologists are aware of a possible post-operative reduction in ovarian function in a small percentage of cases, it seems more likely that the operation is used as the scapegoat for other hostilities and resentments which may be generated within the relationship at a critical life stage.

The husband also is involved in change (or lack of it) in his working life and he may have to acknowledge and accept the approaching years of repetition and tedium which may be ahead of him. His home may need to assume a new and unrealistic importance as a source of alternative activities and interests. There may be a great sense of frustration through a lack of personal and work fulfilment with an associated awareness of lost opportunities to recapture the past. It may be a time when social drinking becomes a firmly entrenched habit and an essential part of the daily routine.

The adaptation may be to move closer within the marital relationship or to take separate diverging paths and form liaisons with others outside the family group. Both courses may provide a satisfactory end result for the individuals concerned, but difficulties arise when there is an emotional stalemate and the individuals become fixed and cling desperately to their old satisfactions and sources of fulfilment. One may see depressive behaviour emerging in response to this interactive stalemate. The old roles become a stereotype and there is an inability to adjust to the changing situation. The depressed mother may then manifest a desperate over protective clinging to her children and an attempt to infantilize them and continue to bind them to herself. She may become increasingly hostile and rejecting of her husband both emotionally, sexually and yet at the same time exhibiting an enormous dependency need for his time and attentions. Lazare and Klerman (1968) examined a consecutive series of 35 depressed women inpatients of which 60% were post-menopausal and found that 43% exhibited largely hysterical symptomatology (with a high level of somatic anxiety and bodily preoccupation especially for gastro-intestinal and genital problems). These women exhibited less in the way of traditional depressive symptoms and they suggested that hysterical personality factors were protecting against depression, and influencing the nature and course of the depressive illness. We would like to suggest that the nature of their symptoms have an interactive and communicative quality which provide secondary gains for the individual as she struggles with her conflict about the nature of her marital relationship at a critical life stage. Lazare and Klerman found a premorbid pattern of an active but unsatisfactory sex life and a medical history marked by expressions of psychic conflicts through marked bodily dysfunction. The hysterical symptomatology and depressive ideas then become the end result of years of emotional unfulfillment and dissatisfactions and arise within the interactive framework of the aging marriage. It suggests also that these women were never very resourceful or adequate in dealing with and accepting the challenges and demands of the trusting and intimate sides of their marriages, but have managed to deal with their earlier conflicts and have decompensated at an age when they interpret their sexuality as increasingly threatened.

In our own study of depressed couples (Hinchliffe, Hooper, Roberts and Vaughan, 1977) we found that we could usefully interpret the results by breaking down the female patients' marriages into those with longstanding marital conflicts and those without. This factor influenced the level of communication they were able to establish with each other by the end of treatment. For the first group we found enduring levels of negative expression and tension and no increase of levels for supportiveness agreement and laughter. Patterns of responsiveness did not vary and levels of acknowledgement of the partners' behaviour did not improve. In the other group they were able to make a better post depressive adjustment to each other and there was a dramatic reduction in their levels of tension and hostility and they seemed to be communicating at an improved level of mutual trust and intimacy.

Our argument has been, therefore, to suggest that the couple who are vulnerable to the stresses of later life stages are also those whose personal adjustments at earlier stages of marriage are less than adequate although to outward appearances the relationship may appear to be a stable one. They are unable to redefine their changed relationship and deal with the new needs and readjustments that become exposed. One must always be aware, therefore, of the subtle disturbances of the balance of the interpersonal relationship and examine behaviour within and across roles.

A discussion of the problems and stresses of the middle years would be incomplete without mentioning the influences of bereavement. Loss during these years is usually of key figures from the previous generations — parents whose existence served a protective reassuring function. Loss of her mother is a major event for the married woman. It impresses upon her the reality of her life stage and increases her sense of vulnerability. She can no longer look forward to the support and understanding of an experienced older woman in the management of her family affairs. It forces her into a new and more independent role in relation to her family group. She may need to turn increasingly to her husband for this comfort that is lacking and this may throw a new emotional strain on the relationship which her partner has problems in meeting. Or alternatively she in her turn may increase her attachment to her daughter or son and look to the next generation for this understanding.

Other writers, Paykel and coworkers (1969) and Leff, Roatch and Bunney (1970) have emphasized the importance of loss in relation to depression. The first writers found an excess of 'exits' amongst the depressives and suggested that the importance of the exit is not in the event itself but in its interactive effect with predisposing vulnerability factors. Leff, Roatch and Bunney found about two-thirds of their male and female subjects had been deprived of a same sex parent in childhood and had lost a model for strong gender identity formation. They described a 'core sensitivity' as a result of childhood losses and bereavements which led to later vulnerability and ill-judged fears for the security of the marital relationship when the partner is absent. In addition they emphasized the greater threat to sexual identity that these core sensitivities might induce.

In another recent paper from his study of women in South London, Brown (1977) has produced more evidence for the sensitizing effects of loss of a mother in childhood and especially before the age of eleven, which he cites as an important factor in influencing the nature of depressions associated with loss in later life. Amongst detailed findings he showed that 66 % of his cases who produced psychotic depressive symptoms had suffered a past loss compared with 39 % who produced neurotic symptoms. For his older psychiatric patients the figures were 45 % and 29.5 % respectively. In addition he demonstrated that loss through death (or effective loss) in the nine months prior to the depression predisposed the individual to psychotic depression, whereas other losses were more likely to produce neurotic depressions. He speculates about the changing sociocultural scene where loss through death in childhood is becoming less common and may influence the pattern of depressive behavior that we are seeing. However, set against this is the greater breakdown of marriage at the present time which may pose another set of problems for the next cohort of women passing through.

Our next case history illustrates some of these points associated with the middle years. A previously capable and effective young woman in her late thirties, presented as depressed, empty, lethargic, with no interest in anything beyond her immediate home and work responsibilities. She had three children who were entering their teens and because of financial pressures to improve their material circumstances she had returned to full-time factory work two years before. Her husband had always been supportive and helpful with the domestic routine, but was feeling increasingly confused and rejected both emotionally and sexually by her behaviour, though admitted that her sexual response had been varied throughout the twenty years of their marriage and that she always tended to be inhibited. However, he had accepted this situation and had always been very fond of his wife. She blamed her hysterectomy of three years before for damaging her sexual response. In fact on looking further into their relationship it became clear that this couple had not established a sufficiently trusting and intimate relationship for them to feel safe to express their anxieties and weaknesses to each other and in fact minimized and dismissed the other whenever attempts were made to look for emotional support and comfort. The patient had a close dependent relationship with her mother and had become involved in her mother's recent depressive illness. She had always derived enormous support from regular visits to her old home. However, since starting work her opportunities for visiting had become limited to the weekend which was the time she had previously spent with her husband. This led to considerable conflict between them until she agreed to curtail her visits. In addition her children were becoming increasingly independent and making less of a demand on her time and emotions. The focus of her life had gradually become centred on her marital relationship and because of her difficulties in trusting and committing herself to this relationship she had taken up a strongly defended and withdrawn position associated with profound feelings of depression and despair. In therapy she slowly acknowledged her need to give up her feelings of hostility and resentment and to realign her present position in the family group.

## Other Critical Years — Old Age and Retirement

Another critical life stage is the social and work withdrawal or retirement phase. One does not read or see much research on the marital problems of this period, but it is another time when depressed behaviour once more emerges as a response to a further period of role redefinition. A new group of people become depressed now, often tending to be vulnerable individuals who have previously been 'worriers' and obsessional personalities but who have adapted to an acceptable life. Then the two elderly people are thrown into close contact with each other in retirement which imposes a strain, not only on the wife's domestic role but also on her husband's as his life becomes very restricted and limited. Once again it is a stage where new alignments must be made, but resourcefulness is required to make a new adjustment to the community in which they are living as it assumes a new importance for them. Longstanding personality problems become exaggerated and they experience difficulties in becoming mutually dependent and supportive. At the same time the couple may exhibit an anxious and hostile concern for the other and make excessive and competitive demands for each other's time and attention which cannot be met and may lead to a depressive episode. As an illustration of these issues we will cite an elderly woman of 70 who had become depressed within the context of her assertive ex-naval husband receiving treatment for carcinoma of the larynx. She gave the impression that she had loathed him for years and had always suffered at his hands and therefore felt little concern for his illness. However, when her husband was seen he made it abundantly clear that he was frightened and concerned for his wife, but that he found her continual demands difficult to tolerate.His illness had caused fear and alarm for both of them and he was very reassured by signs of improvement in his wife.

## Long Term Interactional Effects of Marriage

Turning now to some of the effects on a couple of a troublesome marriage, Kreitman and workers (1970, 1971) and Ovenstone (1973) have all demonstrated the interactive effects of a neurotic male partner on his wife and on the marriage. They found a convergent effect over years of marriage with the wife becoming increasingly like her husband as the marriage lengthened. The severity of the husband's neurosis was considered very important as wives required above average stability to remain well within such a difficult relationship. There were a high proportion of male dominated and segregated marriages present and marital tensions were highest in the segregated group and lowest in the cooperative marriage. These findings support our earlier contention that the vulnerable marriages are those where the early adjustment has been an unsatisfactory one and also suggests that over time the further adaptations that are made do not contribute to the quality of the relationship, but confer a stereotype on the behaviour of both partners.

Pond, Ryle and Hamilton (1963), as a result of their study, suggest the following additional factors are important for marital adjustment:

(1) Age difference between spouses.

(2) Ability to carry on social activities. In the poor marriages the joint activities were very reduced, especially those of the wife.

(3) Decision making and coping with crises. There was a better adjustment where this was a joint activity.

(4) Male dominance. There was a poor adjustment where this was excessive.

Kreitman and coworkers (1970,1971) found similar indications in their study. The neurotic marriages contained more dominant males, there was less role sharing over children and domestic responsibilities and husband and wife spent more time in face to face contact than did the control couples. It is interesting that in the very relationships where the most friction exists, the couples appear to deliberately limit their social contacts and increasingly turn inwards to their own family circle. The underlying anxieties and insecurities of their relationship in fact generate a *greater* dependence for each other and they therefore retain a marked degree of immaturity in their relationship. The more stable marital relationships are able to permit a greater degree of divergence and emotional growth in individual partners, leading to separate interests and activities, thus reinvigorating the marriage by allowing a variety of ideas and range of experiences to be brought back to the home.

These findings for the interactional effects of marriage over time were confirmed in a further study of Hagnell and Kreitman (1974) where the progress of a group of Swedish couples was followed over a ten year period from 1947–1957. By 1957 these couples showed a highly significant excess of conjoint illness over the number to be expected given the original proportions of sick partners. They found the wives were once again particulary at risk and showed a progressive increase in morbidity with years of marriage. The risk of a healthy wife becoming ill is statistically greater than that for the healthy husband of a sick wife, and the illness very frequently takes a depressive form.

## Multiple Stress as a Factor In Marital Depression

Environmental stresses have been blamed as the principle factor in precipitating depression over the years. The introduction of the Holmes and Rahe (1967) Life Event Scale led to a series of papers which examined the principal events leading to depression. It was generally found that marital difficulties ranked high on the list, and the interactive sequelae of the events have been emphasized.

If we move once again to the ideas of the social system we can construe age, length of marriage, social class as the 'givens' of the system and early parental loss, the presence of young children in the home and the quality of the intimate relationship as factors which tune the sensitivity of the system to respond in particular ways to external stresses which disturb the homeostasis of the system suddenly and dramatically. The final outcome is therefore multifactorial in origin and unique to a particular system.

Polak (1971) and Eisler and Polak (1973) amplify this idea and see environmental stresses as disturbing the structure and function of the system by reactivating unresolved conflicts within it. The initial coping patterns within the systen are (a) reality incorporation, (b) expression of feeling, (c) Seeking help, and in the event of all these measures failing, labelling the individual as a patient, thus scapegoating one person and thereby extruding him or her overtly as the cause of the stress. The behaviour which is observed therefore represents a communication about underlying systems conflicts. In their more detailed study Eisler and Polak identified fifteen social system stressors which they defined as social or community events which lead to psychiatric hospitalization of one member of a social system, thus they examined the significance of life events within their wider social setting. They construed the emergence of psychiatric symptoms in one individual as a sign of stress or disturbance in the interactive environment. They say: 'It would appear more likely that stress situations act as general precipitants which may by expressed in varying symptomatology or behavioural disturbance depending on the characteristics of the individual under stress and the resources at his disposal to cope with the stress'.

It is interesting that although they were not primarily considering marital systems in their study, nevertheless their fifteen social system stressors were headed by marital problems. These related mainly to the interaction of the marital pair in relation to communication difficulties, role relationships, dependency, trust and so on. The other stressors ranged over life situations, life stages family relationships and losses and the results showed an average of three social system stressors in the previous two years. When the results were broken down to fit in with the psychiatric diagnosis the depressives came highest for marital problems and also showed a high score for interpersonal problems. Once again these findings underline the association between marital problems and an affective disturbance.

This chapter has dealt with the problem of the aetiology of depression in terms of prior events occurring at various stages of the depressed person's life. We have emphasized throughout the evidence for our interpersonal view of depression as an experience which is itself a system. Our analysis of the data we have presented does enable us to say that the quality of key personal relationships, and especially the marriage, either sustains a competent homeostasis or alternatively leads frequently to a pathological, depressed homeostasis.

Two individuals who maintain distance between themselves and do not allow a reciprocally intimate relationship to develop create long-term problems. The resulting insecurities, misunderstandings and jealousies generate endless incomprehensible mutual rejections which become a stereotyped pattern of need and hostile rejection. This pathological system leads very frequently, we suggest, to the ultimate disturbance of depression.

# 4

# THE PROCESSES OF INTERACTION
# BETWEEN DEPRESSED PATIENTS AND
# THEIR SPOUSES

In this chapter we come to a turning point in our book where we will take a more fundamental look at the processes of interaction for the depressed patient and describe our own research experiences and findings. This will form a link with later chapters in order to give a clearer understanding of the treatment processes involved in tackling the problem of therapy for the depressed patient and partner.

We set out our theoretical reasons for an interpersonal approach to depression in Chapter 1 and now we intend to put some experimental flesh upon the bones of the theory. It may be helpful to repeat that the important framework upon which we base our investigations is that of systems theory. We conceive marriage as a system in which depressive responses become a firm part. They assume a 'message' property which becomes central to the shared experience of both partners. Thus in order to comprehend the pathology of the system we need to define the nature of the communication processes between the partners.

Fortunately other researchers have already made studies of communication in psychiatric patients and we were able to draw on some of their expertise and experience. However most of the work has been done on schizophrenia and in spite of the theoretical criticisms which it raises, has offered a wealth of ideas for theorists and clinicians alike. For a review of these achievements we would refer the interested reader to Hirsch and Leff (1975). The important findings of their research illustrated differential patterns of communication between schizophrenic family members compared with normal family members and such famous descriptive terms as the Double Bind hypothesis (Bateson and his colleagues, 1973). Pseudomutuality (Wynne, 1958) and Marital Schism and Skew (Lidz, 1965) have passed into the psychiatric language. Their findings have created a climate from which other ideas have been able to grow and flourish.

There was little impetus to apply this set of ideas to depression. They had included a developmental theory of family relationships and implied that distorted patterns of communication over years were crucial to psychiatric pathology at a later stage, for the maturing young person. Depression had already been understood in psycho-analytic terms as the response to 'object loss' and this explanation had seemed adequate to explain the phenomena in intrapsychic and intrapersonal terms. An exception to this was the outcome of bereavement studies which were initially based on Freud's formulation. The empirical work showed that the bereavement response related closely to the quality of the prior relationship with the deceased and the grieving process could be modified by the person's interpersonal environment. However, since object loss was central to the events here no further understanding in interpersonal terms was forthcoming.

We understood that depression could be construed in terms of disturbed communication and set within the same theoretical framework as the studies in schizophrenia and this gave us the impetus to begin to see real therapeutic purchase in the interactional view. Initially we applied these ideas to a study of cases of attempted suicide (Roberts and Hooper, 1969) and although we did not assume that they were all necessarily depressed, we looked for distal and proximal causes for their behaviour and found that ruptured personal relationships played a major part in the clinical picture.

Later we pursued the interactional problems of depressed patients by studying their patterns of behaviour in patient–clinician interactions. We focused on the non-verbal qualities of the interaction and measured eye-contact specifically, and also analysed their speech for defensive speech patterns which related to the depressive mood shift (Hinchliffe and coworkers, 1970, 1971). These were aspects of their communication which they, the depressed patients, revealed to others outside their immediate intimate family group. In addition they were influenced by the way they saw the clinician who interviewed them. The results were predictable and illustrated the social retreat and withdrawal characterised by depressed patients. Their speech content revealed greater personal self-preoccupation than controls and greater use of negatives and negatively toned phrases.

We felt that the experimental conditions which we were obliged to impose on the patients produced a very contrived and artificial experience for them and introduced a number of confusing variables. Our aim was to construct a situation where we could sample natural human behaviour in a systematic way. It became important to exclude the therapist as his presence would only disturb and change the very processes we were trying to study.

We had now derived our research model and our next dilemma was to resolve the practical problem of how we would generate a sample of natural interaction for our patient and their spouse which would reveal the depressive-type interaction. We turned once again to the schizophrenic family researchers and decided that we should make a direct observation of husband and wife interacting after they had been set a simple task which would create interaction patterns which were separate from their clinical involvement. This offered better opportunities than other methods where individual family members were asked to produce a sample of some kind of their communication and the individual communications were subjected to a close comparative scrutiny.

**Designing our Study**

We decided to draw on the research techniques and methods which had proved useful in the studies of schizophrenic families carried out by Mishler and Waxler (1968). They had focused on working out an analytic technique for investigating patterns of communication and had derived individual codes so that each would measure some specific aspect of family interaction. The codes could then be grouped together into clusters or domains in order to include the main parameters of human communication. They had drawn the theoretical basis for their codes from the work of a number of family theorists which included Bales' Interaction Process Analysis (I.P.A.) (1951); Mill's Sign Process Analysis (1964); Ruesch's 'Disturbed Communication' (1957); Wynne and Singer's study of 'fragmented communication' (1963); Mahl's studies of speech in relation to anxiety (1956); Goldman-Eisler's (1958) work on 'pauses' and Farina's (1960) studies of 'interruptions'. For the interested reader we would refer them to Mishler and Waxler's book and to our own publications (Hooper, Hinchliffe, Roberts and Vaughan, 1977-8). They were therefore primarily focusing on styles of communication which we felt were crucial to our own approach to depression. Obviously we had no expectation that their observations would bear much relation to our own since they were not only studying a different pathology — schizophrenia — but also studying the triad of mother–father–child (either son or daughter). However, the methods were independent of these differences and had been shown by them to be quite rugged.

Mishler and Waxler generated their family communication by using an earlier technique created by Strodtbeck (1951) to study marital pairs and called the Revealed Difference Technique. This method involves generating a difference of opinion between partners and asking them to discuss their differences. We developed our own 20-item questionnaire by modifying that used by Mishler and Waxler in order to take account of the cultural differences and the fact that we were dealing with a marital pair rather than a family. Each question refers to everyday interpersonal or family experiences which pose a problem, and two alternative outcomes are offered. Each spouse is asked separately to opt for one of the two outcomes and then move on to consider the next problem. Thus, at the conclusion of this exercise the experimenters can examine the husband and wife's individual choices and establish where they are demonstrating a difference of opinion. Then the couple are asked to discuss their differences and attempt to reach an agreement or a disagreement. We found that this proved to be a perfectly satisfactory stimulus for a flow of natural interaction which could then be recorded and analysed.

We decided to record the material on videotape and audiotape so that we would have data for both non-verbal and verbal analysis. We made a preliminary pilot study in order to give the experimenters a chance to develop some expertise with the research method. At times they felt they were developing skills which would equip them for programme presentations on the national network! It was very often necessary to reassure the couple with a preliminary discussion so that they could begin to relax and accept the presence of cameras in the room for the recording.

The couple sat alone in easy chairs in a room by themselves. The television cameras were positioned and left at 'fixed focus' so that there was no need to enter the room during the recording. We used a split-screen unit so that we obtained full face views of each person side by side on the screen. This made the observation of non-verbal behaviour very much easier, although gave an unusual view of a couple interacting. Each couple discussed two or more questions and we made a twenty minute recording of the interaction.

**Selecting a Sample — Psychiatric and Non-Psychiatric**

The problem then, was to carry out a naturalistic study of the depressed patient and his/her spouse in order to study from the record their verbal and non-verbal interaction. We wanted to extend the study and explore other variables related to the problem rather than simply taking a series of psychiatric couples. We decided on three further variables in order to increase the comparisons with our 'core' recording.

First, a recording of the patient going through a similar process of discussion to the one outlined above, but this time with a person of the opposite sex who was strange to them, so that we could check whether the communication pattern was specific to the married pair — an hypothesis which arises directly from our theoretical framework. It seemed important not to involve a psychiatrist who would conduct a formalized interview so we chose a bland interactant of the opposite sex. For this purpose we used a male technician, or a junior nurse unknown to the patient.

Secondly, we compared the couple with themselves at two different points in time, during which the patient was being treated. Our first recording was taken a few days after the patient had been admitted to the Psychiatric Unit and the second one after the patient had been treated, discharged home and was considered recovered by the clinician in charge. This time lapse would obviously vary (with all the methodological problems which that implies) but in fact ranged between three to twelve months.

Finally we compared the depressed couple with a 'normal' couple. We decided that in order to make a fair comparison we must repeat the separation and hospitalization experience of our psychiatric couples. Therefore we chose surgical patients admitted for minor surgical procedures and specifically excluded patients who had a long medical or surgical history or any disorder with strong psychological connections such as gastric or duodenal ulcers and neoplastic conditions. We screened them for any history of psychiatric disturbance or major marital conflict. Unfortunately we were not able to repeat the follow-up recording with our control couples.

In an ideal study the couples would have been both unselected (except in terms of the research criteria) and would have included the total sample of those who had been asked to participate. Unfortunately in real-life clinical research it is not as easy as that, and there are obvious shortfalls in the number of patients who can be persuaded to take part. This was especially true of a videotape study which posed too threatening a demand for some people especially when they were in an emotionally vulnerable state. For a ground-breaking study like this one these discrepancies are more acceptable than in later repetitive studies, but it is important to set down what these were so that the reader can judge the weight which he is ultimately willing to put upon the data. The details of the selective process are therefore shown in Table 4.1 along with some simple demographic data and demonstrates the difficulty which we had in recruiting a sample of surgical patients and spouses. Nearly half the patients interviewed either refused to take part, or were unable to enlist the cooperation of their partners, or were discharged before we could make the technical arrangements for the recording. As the recording of the surgical couples proceeded we tried to match them with one of our psychiatric couples and this, too, meant increasing difficulty as the choice had to be more selective. The factors we were especially concerned with here were social class, length of marriage and presence or absence of children.

**Table 4.1**
*Selection of subjects and details of sample*

|  | Psychiatric | Surgical |
| --- | --- | --- |
| Total number initial interview | 46 | 84 |
| Unsuitable | 13 | 24 |
| Suitable but refused or unable | 13 | 20 |
| No record through technical or administrative problems | 5 | 19 |
| Initial Recording | 20 | 20 |
| Follow-up Recording | 17 | Not applicable |
| Patient — Male | 8 | 10 |
| Female | 12 | 10 |
| Age range | 26–61 | 25–58 |
| mean | 42.5 | 42.0 |
| Zung Depression Score |  |  |
| mean initial | 67% | 35% |
| mean follow-up | 52% | Not applicable |
| Length of marriage (mean years) | 18 | 20 |
| Social Class I | 2 | 3 |
| II | 3 | 9 |
| III | 10 | 6 |
| IV | 2 | 2 |
| V | 3 | 0 |
| Children — (Absent) | 4 | 5 |
| — (Present) | 16 | 15 |

The psychiatric patients were mostly drawn from a small acute treatment unit containing thirty beds and located in a general hospital. A small number were also taken from an acute treatment unit in a neighbouring psychiatric hospital. They were initially selected on the basis of a diagnosis of depression given by a hospital psychiatrist which was subsequently confirmed (or not) by Mary Hinchliffe. At this confirmatory stage we also excluded any patient with a history of alcoholism, brain damage, or schizophrenic disorder. Finally, each patient completed the Zung

Depression Self-Rating Scale (Zung, 1965) and we used 60% as our cut-off score for depression. The surgical patients also completed the Zung Scale and the mean scores for both groups are also shown in Table 4.1. We made no attempt in either sample to try and create a group with specifically 'good' marriages. This was not really possible after a single interview with the surgical patients. This may be seen as vitiating any subsequent comparison, but we rejected this argument on the grounds that the important discriminations would be within the depressed sample, and for these couples we did have the information to make a judgement of their marriage.

## The Psychiatric Sample

We have now described the theoretical basis of our study and given details about our sample and the technical method we used in order to sample the behaviour of individual couples. At this point we would like to introduce the reader to some of the clinical details of two contrasting couples from the study in order to give more idea of the flavour and background of our couples. Our later discussion will be in terms of differences between all the couples treated as dyads, so this is the place to redress that imbalance by concentrating on the individual couples themselves. One must emphasize, however, that no one couple can be representative of anything but themselves, but the descriptions will at least clothe the concept of 'depressed couple' with meaning. In each case the identifying details have been removed but the important themes within their lives are as accurate as possible.

The first pair are Mr. and Mrs. L who were an attractive young couple in their late twenties. They have a two-year old son and lived in a small flat. Mr. L was the depressed spouse who had experienced longstanding feelings of personal inadequacy. He was a trained engineer by profession and had recently been given a supervisory role with responsibility for a number of subordinates. This had increased his perception of himself as inadequate although this was far from apparent superficially. He struggled to present an integrated 'front' to the world even in the psychiatric unit. This struggle had now become impossible for him to maintain at work or at home, but hospitalization had not released him from the need to continue to struggle. Prior to the present disturbance the couple appeared to have had a good, relatively conflict free complementary relationship, but one in which the roles were rather rigidly defined and probably with a good deal of anxious behaviour. Mrs. L was a cheerful, friendly, straightforward young woman with few apparent problems of her own. In the presence of her husband her style shifted to one of considerable tension and anxious concern. The birth of their son seems to have been a major event which altered the balance of their marital style. From the description which they give, Mrs. L probably withdrew a lot of her emotional support from her husband at this time and is now quite preoccupied with the problem of mothering a toddler. Mr. L's resentment at this shift in his wife's emotional investment is apparent in his current preoccupations; although he denies any awareness of these difficulties, he now feels that he has lost control in two major sectors of his world with massive implications for his own self-esteem. He was an in-patient for three weeks and treated with anti-depressant medication and the couple were interviewed jointly. He derived considerable help from both treatment regimes and they re-established a more stable family relationship and were much more relaxed and cheerful by the second recording.

The second couple are one of the older pairs in the sample. Mrs. R is the one who is depressed and who, despite considerable despair, manages to keep herself looking 'nice'. They are both in their mid-fifties and appear superficially to be a very solid couple. They are childless and live in a pleasant flat. Mr. R is a sales manager in a large commercial firm and enjoys the social life which his job brings him. They seem in the past to have had a relatively immature relationship, spent most of their leisure time together and enjoyed indulging each other with material possessions. She, for her part, was very anxious to have approval and praise from others and easily adopted a dependent role towards them. But towards her husband she became very hostile and critical as she felt more depressed. He dealt with this fairly unsuccessfully by trying to assist her in the home and offer her kindly reassurances. Yet somehow his overtures lacked real warmth, as if he knew what effect he wished to achieve but did not have the resources to be convincing. Thus the overall impression is of two immature people (despite appearances to the contrary) who have very few resources to meet the present difficulties. There is also more than a hint that her hostility has been increasing in the marriage for a long while and that she is achieving some secondary gain from the present disturbance. Certainly the present relationship structure was probably a good deal more complementary than anything which they had achieved in the past, but potentially destructive. The current difficulties for Mr. and Mrs. R appear to have started in relation to Mrs. R's discovery that Mr. R had a warm close relationship with a younger woman in his office. She made a slow response to E.C.T. and anti-depressant medication and at 'follow-up' was still demonstrating considerable tension and hostility towards her husband, who was becoming less tolerant and more challenging than hitherto. She was feeling better and able to return to her part-time job, however.

These two couples exemplify some of the problems of each of the other couples forming the psychiatric sample. There was often a good deal of covert conflict and resentment which does appear in the study material. Sometimes this seemed to be because the marriage had been constructed in a way which had personally disabled one partner and thus the depressive pattern included a decompensatory process in relation to this. For others this was not so apparent, and the relationship appeared to have adapted to the distressed spouse in a way that was more nurturing. This seemed to be more true of the couples in which the husband was the patient rather than the wife. One needs to take the previous quality of the marriage into account. On a global assessment, the female patients' marriages seemed less happy and effective previously than those of the male patients. Our case study exemplifies this point. Some of our observations must be interpreted with this in mind. It is also important to remember that our reconstruction of their previous relationship is dependent on their own accounts of themselves at a time when their marriages are under strain.

**Analysing the Interaction**

At least these vignettes have given some flavour to what must inevitably be a rather dehumanized account of the process of interaction. The reality of the phenomena we seek must lie beneath the kaleidoscopic surface of human communication and will necessarily require some abstraction to capture them. So if the couples which are described above are borne in mind these abstractions can be restored, as it were, to the level of human experience again.

What data did we actually have to analyse? In fact, it was the product ultimately of four recording sessions which were as follows:

Session 1. Depressed patient and spouse in hospital
Session 2. Depressed patient and stranger of opposite sex in hospital
Session 3. Recovered patient and spouse recorded back in hospital
Session 4. Surgical patient and spouse in hospital

It took more than two years to collect the data from the first pilot sessions until the last session of the 'recovered' couples had been completed. At the end of each video recording session, the stereo sound tape was produced and these audio recordings (80 in all) were transcribed. Each transcription was then checked against the tape and particular importance was paid to ensuring that all ungrammatical constructions, speech fragments and overlying speech had been reproduced on the typescript and not 'cleaned up' by the typist. The scripts were then divided into communicative acts according to the system developed by Mishler and Waxler who define a communicative act as the smallest unit of meaningful speech. In most cases this is a clause with subject and predicate either present or implied, although it can often be a single word such as 'yes' or 'good' which was quite clearly meaningful as an act, although not grammatically complete. In Sessions 1, 3 and 4 a total of 400 acts were coded for each couple. This is equivalent to about 20 minutes of the interaction and was selected from the last section of the tape after the warming-up period. In Session 2 which is the record of the patient with a stranger only 200 acts were coded because the records were very consistent and this proved to be an adequate sample.

The next step was to apply a series of codes to these acts so that we produced a total score for the presence of various characteristics in the scripts. For example, the emotional tone of the words used for each act formed an important part of the communication and the score for a participant would then consist of the percentage of acts which had carried positive, negative, and neutral affect. Finally, the codes were collated together into communicative domains which were the major area for analysis and are based on complex but meaningful areas of human communication. These need to be described in some detail since they form the basis of intergroup comparison and they are all derived from Mishler and Waxler's study.

The four domains are:
1. EXPRESSIVENESS This domain deals with the emotional tone of the communicative acts of each participant. The acts are coded with reference both to the language used and also to the tone of voice.

2. RESPONSIVENESS Here the observer is concerned with the levels of acknowledgement in the response patterns and also the focus of response of each partner. This is therefore a properly interactive measure and although each person's responsiveness is considered separately, the codes take into account the stimulus properties of the prior messages. Lack of adequate responsiveness obviously diminishes communication — a factor of considerable theoretical importance in depression.

3. DISRUPTIONS The communicative sequence has a pattern of its own which is characterized by the way it is broken up. There are a number of ways in which this occurs, such as by laughter, long pauses and sentence fragments. The title 'disruptions' almost implies a value judgement, but obviously natural communication is disrupted. The less disrupted the communication the more formal it becomes.

4. POWER Finally, the question of differential control of the process of interaction is an important one and this is what is meant by the domain of power. It can usefully be divided into control over the focus of attention and the control which one partner exercises over the response of the other. These are known as attention control and person control respectively.

These domains were constructed by applying eleven separate codes to each act or unit of measurement in the protocol, and therefore individually represent the collating of a group of codes. It would be tedious to set out each of these codes in detail — the interested reader can find full details in the associated research papers (Hooper and coworkers, 1977), (Hinchliffe and coworkers 1977) but a list of the eleven codes will show the areas which were covered. They were:

Affect
Bales' I.P.A.
Acknowledgement  Stimulus
                 Response
Focus
Fragments — Incomplete sentences
            Word/phrase repetition
            Unclear/incomplete phrases
            Laughter
Pauses
Interruptions

Each code has a series of rules which the coder follows in deciding which category each unit of interaction should fall into.

## Non-verbal communication

The videotape method also gave us the opportunity to examine the interaction along quite different lines from the verbal content. Here we were forced to adapt our methods of analysis from other research contexts which were not so directly

**Table 4.2**

*Sample verbal communication analysis*

| | *Couple Analysis & Sessions* | | | | *Roles & Sessions* | | | | | *Roles within Sessions (significant results only)* | | | |
|---|---|---|---|---|---|---|---|---|---|---|---|---|---|
| | 1 | 2 | 3 | 4 | | 1 | 2 | 3 | 4 | 1 | 2 | 3 | 4 |
| Couples | | X | X | X | All male | X | X | X | X | | | | |
| | | | | | All female | X | X | X | X | | | | |
| | | | | | All patients | X | X | X | X | | | | |
| | | | | | All non-patients | X | X | X | X | | | | |
| | | | | | Male patients | X | X | X | X | Males | | | |
| | | | | | Spouse | X | X | X | X | v | | | |
| | | | | | Female Patients | X | X | X | X | Females | | | |
| | | | | | Spouse | X | X | X | X | (etc.) | | | Female Patients v Spouses (etc.) |

X = Mean figure expressed as percentage.

applicable to our data. We also had to choose which areas of behaviour were most appropriate for our purposes, but without being able to call on any previous studies in depression. We decided to study hand movements, posture, and eye-gaze. Hand movements have been described by others in terms of body-focused movements and object-focused movements (Friedman and Hoffman, 1967). Depressed patients exhibited greater use of inturned or '*body-focused*' movements and made little use of outward turned or communicative gestures, described as *object-focused*. Posture was different in that the interesting thing was congruence or matching of posture between the couple. Charney's (1969) work was particularly important in showing that congruency seemed to go with positive, specific, interpersonal communication. We found that well matched control couples took up symmetrical positions in their chairs and followed each other's postural changes. Finally, eye-gaze seemed such a classical aspect of depressed behaviour that it should be included. It has attracted surprisingly little research although we had done some exploratory work ourselves (Hinchliffe and coworkers, 1970–1971).

In this chapter we can only report the results of part of this non-verbal analysis since it is still continuing, but the data on eye-gaze are complete together with the whole of the verbal analysis of material. However the results represent an incredibly large number of detailed decisions about the minute aspects of the couples' behaviour, since there were 28,000 acts for analysis. We therefore ran reliability checks on random samples of the coded data and found that this was at least 90 % in all the codes in use except for the I.P.A. code of Bales. Here, coding was consistently lower and reached 75 % agreement although all cases of discrepant coding were resolved by subsequent discussion.

The most important results will be presented here, and Table 4.2 shows the way in which the verbal communication data was handled for each code within each domain. We made both couple and individual comparisons and did this within sessions and across the four sessions. Thus we compared the combined results of one couple with another and looked at individual differences in a session and compared this with the other different interactional situations under study. We defined roles within the study and made interrole comparisons, e.g. males with females, psychiatric patients with non-psychiatric patients, husbands with wives etc. Thus we made intercouple, interindividual and intraindividual comparisons.

We have outlined the most important findings by simplifying the comparisons and have summarized the data to the eight Tables 4.3 to 4.10. Tests of statistical significance were applied to each pair of observations and to show where these reached certain confidence levels, we have used a simple notation. Whenever the value of P was 0.05 or less we have joined the two figures with a blocked line and wherever the value was 0.1 or less (and thus indicates a trend) the figures are joined with a dotted line. Since our emphasis is upon the couples, the tables that seem most appropriate are those which deal with the comparison of the marital pairs in each session drawn from the larger mass of data. Each domain of communication will be dealt with separately and the appropriate data presented for the reader to consider in the light of our discussion of the findings.

## Research Findings — Expressiveness

The most important finding confirms our predictions that the depressed couples show considerably more expressiveness both as individuals and as a couple than do the others. Also one of the most marked features is the sharp difference between Sessions 1 and 2 which are those in which the depressed person switches from his/ her partner to a stranger. Each table for Expressiveness demonstrates this change and seems to show that the depressed communicative style varies with context and is just not consistent from one individual to another. This is a major finding which occurs not only in this domain but in all the others — as we shall see. The general measure of expressiveness is broken up into positive and negative aspects in Tables 4.4 and 4.5. Returning to the couples, we can see that there are marked differences for negative expressiveness. Here too, another of the important general findings of the research emerges which is the differences between the depressed men and their wives and the depressed women and their husbands. Table 4.4 shows that the negative communication is at about the same level for patient and spouse alike, but that by Session 3 (i.e. recovery) the pattern between the male patient couples is very similar to that of the surgical men and wives, whereas the depressed women show little change compared with their husbands.

The table giving data on the Affect scale (which is a narrower rating of the expressive characteristic) demonstrates rather the same thing, with the depressed men and their wives using affective communication markedly more in the acute depressed situation than in either the recovery situation or when compared with their surgical counterparts. However there is little change for the depressed women and their husbands. It is interesting that we have shown a change in the pattern of the means for these couples in the direct measure of expressiveness (see above). One can suggest that they have demonstrated a change in the music of their communication by recovery, but have not changed the words being used. The non-verbal patterns have greater meaning and underline the importance of our earlier comment that feeling may be expressed covertly in many of our couples. Perhaps

**Table 4.3**
*General expressiveness*

| Person | Session | | | |
|---|---|---|---|---|
| | 1 | 2 | 3 | 4 |
| Couple | 50 | 35 | 41 | 43 |
| Male Patient | 50 | | 34 | 34 |
| Spouse | 52 | | 50 | 52 |
| Female Patient | 47 | | 44 | 46 |
| Spouse | 51 | | 37 | 39 |

**Table 4.4**
*Negative expressiveness*

| Person | Session | | | |
|---|---|---|---|---|
| | 1 | 2 | 3 | 4 |
| Couple | 30 | 11 | 24 | 19 |
| Male Patient | 28 | | 13 | 16 |
| Spouse | 25 | | 19 | 19 |
| Female Patient | 31 | | 28 | 24 |
| Spouse | 36 | | 22 | 16 |

**Table 4.5**
*Positive expressiveness*

| Person | Session | | | |
|---|---|---|---|---|
| | 1 | 2 | 3 | 4 |
| Couple | 20 | 24 | 17 | 24 |
| Male Patient | 21 | | 22 | 18 |
| Spouse | 26 | | 28 | 33 |
| Female Patient | 16 | | 15 | 21 |
| Spouse | 15 | | 14 | 22 |

**Table 4.6**
*Affect*

| Person | Session | | | |
|---|---|---|---|---|
| | 1 | 2 | 3 | 4 |
| Couple | 50 | 41 | 42 | 46 |
| Male Patient | 51 | | 44 | 40 |
| Spouse | 51 | | 43 | 48 |
| Female Patient | 47 | | 45 | 46 |
| Spouse | 43 | | 43 | 43 |

**Table 4.7**
*Negative tension*

| Person | Session | | | |
|---|---|---|---|---|
| | 1 | 2 | 3 | 4 |
| Couple | 14 | 6 | 9 | 3 |
| Male Patient | 20 | | 7 | 5 |
| Spouse | 12 | | 4 | 1 |
| Female Patient | 13 | | 14 | 4 |
| Spouse | 14 | | 10 | 5 |

**Table 4.8**
*Positive tension*

| Person | Session | | | |
|---|---|---|---|---|
| | 1 | 2 | 3 | 4 |
| Couple | 2 | 3 | 5 | 5 |
| Male Patient | 2 | | 5 | 6 |
| Spouse | 3 | | 9 | 6 |
| Female Patient | 1 | | 2 | 3 |
| Spouse | 2 | | 3 | 5 |

**Table 4.9**
*Negative interpersonal expressiveness*

| Person | Session | | | |
|---|---|---|---|---|
| | 1 | 2 | 3 | 4 |
| Couple | 7 | 2 | 3 | 5 |
| Male Patient | 4 | | 3 | 5 |
| Spouse | 1 | | 6 | 9 |
| Female Patient | 10 | | 4 | 10 |
| Spouse | 14 | | 5 | 3 |

**Table 4.10**
*Positive interpersonal expressiveness*

| Person | Session | | | |
|---|---|---|---|---|
| | 1 | 2 | 3 | 4 |
| Couple | 7 | 2 | 9 | 8 |
| Male Patient | 6 | | 9 | 8 |
| Spouse | 8 | | 8 | 7 |
| Female Patient | 2 | | 5 | 9 |
| Spouse | 6 | | 13 | 8 |

surprisingly, the depressed couples do not increase their levels of positive expressiveness at recovery and indeed it is reduced overall, but with a good deal of variance, as the statistic shows.

The two tables dealing with the tension aspects of communication (which is largely measured paralinguistically) also show a general drop in negative tension although again not in the case of the depressed female pairs. The final tables deal with the use of interpersonal expression and the differences between all three samples are less here.

Our general conclusions are that expressiveness tends to be high in the depressed couples and falls to the level of the surgical couples by recovery, but with sharp differences for the patterns of the male marriages and the female marriages. The key to understanding the differences between the two may lie in the fact that when the male is disturbed and depressed there is a much greater shift in his behaviour from the instrumental to the expressive mode. This may initially play a major part in disturbing the equilibrium in the marriage, but at recovery the change in behaviour is more clearcut and offers more reassurance to the spouse. In comparison, the female patient's partner becomes expressive and supportive to meet her disturbances and experiences great difficulty in returning to his more instrumental role at recovery. The wife may enjoy her new found dependent role and make a continued demand for it. One can speculate that it may be in the interest of the stability of the marriage for the husband to actually do the reverse of this, and maintain his instrumental style in a more stable fashion. It looks as if the role shift which certainly occurs with depression is easier for wives of patients rather than husbands and that the regressive dependent behaviour of the men more easily shifts back again. It would be interesting to study the specific patterns of dependent males who are less motivated to affect this role shift and find the more instrumental role a challenging one.

### Responsiveness

The codes which are used in this domain aim to capture the attentiveness and mutuality within the communicative style of the couples. Human communication continues only so long as one individual responds to the other in some way, and each partner is properly responsive when he not only attends to the content and intention of his partner, but also responds to it in his own way. The classical view of the depressed person is that he is unable to do this because of his self-centred apathy. In their work, Mishler and Waxler (1968) showed — contrary to their expectations — that the normal family members were mutually responsive, but also with a good deal of fragmentary communication and unevenness and thus the communication tended to be 'untidy' as compared with the formal tidiness of the disturbed families. The codes which we demonstrate here deal with both the reciprocity of the partners and also the content of the communication and the type of referents which are used. Selected results are shown numerically in Tables 4.11 to 4.16 and give the more important and interesting findings.

**Table 4.11**
*Responsiveness — positive acknowledgement*

| Person | Session | | | |
|---|---|---|---|---|
| | 1 | 2 | 3 | 4 |
| Couples | 90 | 95 | 89 | 89 |
| Male Patient | 89 | | 87 | 85 |
| Spouse | 90 | | 88 | 88 |
| Female Patient | 90 | | 92 | 94 |
| Spouse | 90 | | 91 | 89 |

**Table 4.12**
*Responsiveness — fragmented communication*

| Person | Session | | | |
|---|---|---|---|---|
| | 1 | 2 | 3 | 4 |
| Couple | 27 | 36 | 32 | 32 |
| Male Patient | 35 | | 29 | 38 |
| Spouse | 29 | | 32 | 26 |
| Female Patient | 22 | | 29 | 32 |
| Spouse | 24 | | 39 | 33 |

**Table 4.13**

*Responsiveness — focus on situation*

| Person | Session | | | |
|---|---|---|---|---|
| | 1 | 2 | 3 | 4 |
| Couple | 5 | 3 | 5 | 6 |
| Male Patient | 6 | | 4 | 8 |
| Spouse | 3.5 | | 6.5 | 7 |
| Female Patient | 4 | | 3 | 6 |
| Spouse | 7.5 | | 6 | 6 |

**Table 4.14**

*Responsiveness — focus on personal experience*

| Person | Session | | | |
|---|---|---|---|---|
| | 1 | 2 | 3 | 4 |
| Couple | 26 | 25 | 25 | 16 |
| Male Patient | 23 | | 24 | 15 |
| Spouse | 26 | | 21 | 13 |
| Female Patient | 28 | | 33 | 19 |
| Spouse | 25 | | 21 | 14 |

**Table 4.15**

*Responsiveness — 'I' as subject*

| Person | Session | | | |
|---|---|---|---|---|
| | 1 | 2 | 3 | 4 |
| Couple | 49 | 48 | 49 | 56 |
| Male Patient | 51 | | 55 | 46 |
| Spouse | 43 | | 46 | 53 |
| Female Patient | 55 | | 53 | 52 |
| Spouse | 42 | | 43 | 44 |

**Table 4.16**
*Responsiveness — 'you' as subject*

| Person | Session | | | |
|---|---|---|---|---|
| | 1 | 2 | 3 | 4 |
| Couple | 16 | 16 | 14 | 10 |
| Male Patient | 15 | | 12 | 7 |
| Spouse | 14 | | 19 | 9 |
| Female Patient | 15 | | 15 | 12 |
| Spouse | 20 | | 19 | 12 |

The first table shows that there are few differences between the sessions and that the levels of acknowledgement are pretty uniform, but the second table does reveal some differences. The depressed couples use less fragmentation and *are* more orderly in their communication; although this changes quite sharply and fragmentation is increased when they are talking with the stranger. This characteristic is also much more marked for the depressed women and husbands than for the men and their wives. But unlike the findings in the domain of expressiveness, the depressed wives and their spouses become like their surgical counterparts at the recovery session.

Tables 4.13 and 4.14 give us some idea of the degree to which the couples differ in the focus of the interactional content. Their use of the situational context is not very different, although the normal couples are more symmetrical in this than the depressed couples, the depressed women showing the lowest scores here. But the use of personal experience shows sharp differences. The psychiatric couples are far more likely to use their personal experience but also to do this reciprocally, and this tends to remain their style. They relate the anonymous family situations they were asked to discuss to their own experience, whilst the surgical pairs are happy to discuss the situations in terms of the issues involved rather than themselves. This was quite striking whilst listening to the tapes, and confirms the clinical view that the depressive world is essentially a self-centred one.

This is in contrast with the use which the couples make of themselves as referent, In both depressed males and females, there is significantly more use of the personal pronoun than in their partners, but they are not very different in this respect from the surgical couples. Where they do differ is in referring to their spouse with the use of 'you' and here they tend to have much higher scores. The coding discriminates between the use of 'you' when referring to the other and 'you' when it is used in the third person, and this Table is the use of the former style. Couples demonstrate a degree of reciprocity and they are once again much more involved with the personal preoccupations of their ongoing relationship and are less able to be objective and use 'you' in the third person as do the controls. The use of 'we' which we have not shown in detail here supports the same style with the depressed couples making rather more use of this address than the surgical pairs.

The general results from our examination of this area of communication suggest that the depressed couple are still very responsive to each other although we might have expected otherwise. Mishler and Waxler suggest that acknowledgement levels must be around 90% to enable communication to proceed, and these are the levels which we have observed in our study. The highest level, indeed, being that produced by the depressed patient/stranger couple which speaks of an interpersonal sensitivity considerably greater than clinical observation would sometimes suggest. But the depressed couples also show a significantly greater formality of style than their surgical comparisons, and give some support to the idea of a shift here which is related to the depressive communication. Further examination reveals that this is, again, a particular characteristic of the female patients rather than the males, but that in both cases the pattern seems to be normal by the recovery period.

In terms of the personal and situational referents which are used, we have found what we might have expected, which is that the communication is much more personalized for the depressed couples than for the others, and this is confirmed by analysis of other data from the study. The heightened responsiveness shown by the use of personal 'you' is quite surprising, but perhaps goes along with the more formal 'turn-taking' style of speech which we observed. This certainly has to be borne in mind in the light of the findings which we reviewed above on expressiveness.

### Disruptions of Speech

Disruptions may seem a strange phenomenon to study in communication, but they are in fact a most important part of the process. It is a particularly important area when we are discussing depressed individuals because the disrupted speech of the patient has been one of the classical ways to clinically evaluate the individual. To take only two of the phenomena involved, slow speech rate and long pauses in speech are both thought to be important indicators of the depressed response. Now obviously all speech needs both pattern and variety, and disruptions are the mechanism by which this can occur. In the flow of interaction there need to be changes from time to time in order to introduce new ideas or regroup old ones. Inevitably points of tension also arise and need to be expressed by paralinguistic means as well as by words. There must also be an absolute limit to disruptions or else communication will be seriously impeded.

A number of different kinds of disruption can be measured in human communication, and we will consider here the most obvious ones. We have already mentioned the release of tension, and by this we mean the occurrence of stuttering, repetitions, laughter and joking which have been used by a number of other researchers to indicate the presence of difficulty within the communicative process. Pauses are also important, and their presence is defined by the listening coder when he judges that a longer break than is characteristic for the couple has occurred. Laughter — which we might expect to be significantly less in the depressed couples

68

— is the last indicator that we shall discuss. Once again some of these data are summarized in Tables 4.17 to 4.21 to include the most interesting of the research measures.

The first three tables which are used to describe this domain deal with tension (both positive and negative). In general the depressed couples show much higher rates of this kind of communicative act exhibited by tense emotional outbursts and once again we observed the sharp reduction in the 'depressed' communication style when the patient was interacting with the stranger. Male patients have the highest overall rate of tension release, but this reduces sharply by the recovery session. In comparison, neither depressed women, nor the wives of depressed men alter significantly between the hospitalized and the recovery sessions. Looking down the figures, the depressed couples obviously need tension releasers less by the time they are more normal, but they still show evidence of more tension than the control couples.

**Table 4.17**
*Disruptions — tension release*

| Person | Session | | | |
|---|---|---|---|---|
| | 1 | 2 | 3 | 4 |
| Couple | 17 | 10 | 14 | 9 |
| Male Patients | 23 | | 13 | 11 |
| Spouse | 16 | | 13 | 7 |
| Female Patients | 14 | | 16 | 8 |
| Spouse | 17 | | 15 | 9 |

**Table 4.18**
*Disruptions — positive tension release*

| Person | Session | | | |
|---|---|---|---|---|
| | 1 | 2 | 3 | 4 |
| Couple | 2 | 3 | 5 | 5 |
| Male Patients | 2 | | 5 | 6 |
| Spouse | 3 | | 9 | 6 |
| Female Patients | 1 | | 2 | 3 |
| Spouse | 2 | | 3 | 5 |

**Table 4.19**
*Disruptions — negative tension release*

| Person | Session 1 | 2 | 3 | 4 |
|---|---|---|---|---|
| Couples | 14 | 6 | 8 | 3 |
| Male Patients | 20 | | 7 | 5 |
| Spouse | 12 | | 4 | 1 |
| Female Patients | 13 | | 14 | 4 |
| Spouse | 14 | | 10 | 5 |

**Table 4.20**
*Disruptions — laughter*

| Person | Session 1 | 2 | 3 | 4 |
|---|---|---|---|---|
| Couples | 1 | 2 | 2 | 2 |
| Male Patients | 0.5 | | 1 | 1 |
| Spouse | 2 | | 5 | 2.5 |
| Female Patients | 0.5 | | 1 | 2 |
| Spouse | 1.5 | | 1 | 2 |

**Table 4.21**
*Disruptions — Pauses*

| Person | Session 1 | 2 | 3 | 4 |
|---|---|---|---|---|
| Couples | 4 | 2 | 2 | 1.5 |
| Male Patients | 6 | | 3 | 1 |
| Spouse | 4 | | 3 | 1 |
| Female Patients | 4 | | 2 | 1 |
| Spouse | 5 | | 1 | 1 |

When we examine the contributions of positive and negative tension releasers in the next two tables, it is evident where the major differences are between the two sets of couples. The measures of negative tension are extremely high for the depressed couples and once more the female patients are marked out by the absence of change at the recovery session. The surgical couples show a fairly even balance between positive and negative tension and obviously use both rather than one or the other. The depressed couples demonstrate a seven-fold difference between positive and negative tension in Session 1, whereas the difference for the surgical pairs is not even two-fold — and then in the reverse direction. The male patients and their wives show a clearcut increase in their use of positive tension releasers by recovery, suggesting that the use of humour is a feature of a well-adjusted relationship.

Our final tables in this section deal with pauses in speech and with the occurrence of laughter. The reader will see that we failed to find the expected differences in the occurrence of laughter and the measures are uniformly low. There seems to be no obvious explanation of this, although it would be tempting to see the laughter of the depressed men's wives in Session 3 as marking their relief! The measure of pauses does fulfil the expectation for considerably decreased flow of speech at the time of the acute depressive experience. The differences are quite uniform for all the sub-classes which we have considered, and although they do not necessarily reach significance, there is a distinct drop in the number of pauses between Session 1 and 3. The fascinating aspect of this observation is that the spouse of the depressed patient adapts to the other partner so that the style remains a very symmetrical one, and that this symmetry is maintained by each of the couples in each of the sessions (including the stranger/patient interaction although we have not shown all the data here).

These results are somewhat contrary to the observations which Mishler and Waxler made on the schizophrenic families. As a result of their work they suggested that high levels of disruption were associated with healthy relationships, but our findings suggest that a very high rate can be the pathological equivalent for depressed patients of a very low rate in schizophrenic families. On the basis of our results, we would say that depressed communication has a negative and uneven flow, but one which is apparently reversible in view of the different pattern which depressed patients show with the strangers. Here the pause rate is halved, and the laughter rate is doubled, indicating that these characteristics of speech disruption are generated by the interaction and not just a characteristic of a depressed 'state'

**Power**

Finally we want to consider certain measures of power in the communication. In some ways influence or control would be better terms to describe the area we are now turning to, but since power is the term used by Mishler and Waxler we will use it here, but ask the reader to bear in mind our preferred terms. In the family setting the exercise of power is likely to be more open than in the marital setting, although here, too, it is a most important, though more subtle, factor. It seems likely that relative power is determined quite early in any relationship, but that it may change as the roles within the relationship change. For example, the youthful submissive wife may become the much more dominant mother and wife-partner after a decade or so and psychological disturbance might result in an erstwhile dominant husband becoming quite dependent as he feels less competent. Indeed, the depressive experience itself often seems to be the response to a power conflict in which the person struggles to maintain a position after a major loss of some kind. Among women, at least, there is evidence from Weissman and Paykel (1974) that a clear factor of submissive dependency emerges with the full development of depressive patterns.

Methods of exercising control and of responding to it will be quite varied, but in our study we examined the techniques which individuals used to gain attention for themselves by controlling their rate of speech and length of statement. We have also examined the degree of confrontation which is shown directly by interruptions of the other person, and less directly by questioning. It is possible to construe the depressive stance as itself an attempt to exercise metacontrol over the situation, but this is not possible to identify in the couples using our present methods. To counteract this, we can invoke a non-verbal method to shed some light on to the whole situation in the form of a measure of eye-gaze. Gaze serves both an expressive and a regulatory function and differs between the sexes. In ordinary contact eye-gaze has been found to mark the beginning and end of statements, and also to be avoided where verbal intimacy increases. We have no prior way of knowing how gaze would be used by our couples, although we expected it might well *increase* or *decrease* in relation to the surgical couples, and also show the usual sexual differences. The important variables in this domain are laid out in Tables 4.22. to 4.26 although much of the detailed observations have been omitted from this account.

The first table contains the surprising observation that for the subjects we investigated, the differences in mutual speech rate appeared in the recovery session and not in the initial hospital session. Despite this, the surgical couples still have higher speech rates than the depressed couples at either session, but with this anomaly of difference. Consideration of statement length does not really clarify this observation much, because again the differences are more marked by Session 3 than between Sessions 1 and 4. As a measure of control, therefore, these data did not prove very illuminating. The other data on person control are more helpful, and the details of attempted interruptions are particularly interesting. Here we see that the

**Table 4.22**
*Power — attention control (speech rate)*

| Person | Session | | | |
|---|---|---|---|---|
| | 1 | 2 | 3 | 4 |
| Male patient Couples | 154 | | 151 | 166 |
| Female patients Couples | 163 | | 156 | 175 |
| All couples | 159 | | 153 | 171 |

**Table 4.23**
*Power — attention control (statement length)*

| Person | Session | | | |
|--------|---|---|---|---|
| | 1 | 2 | 3 | 4 |
| Male Patient | 3 | | 6 | 4 |
| Spouse | 3 | | 3 | 3 |
| Female Patient | 3.5 | | 4 | 3 |
| Spouse | 3 | | 5 | 4 |

**Table 4.24**
*Power — attempted interruptions*

| Person | Session | | | |
|--------|---|---|---|---|
| | 1 | 2 | 3 | 4 |
| Couples | 8.5 | 5 | 6 | 7 |
| Male Patients | 7 | | 5 | 6 |
| Spouse | 11 | | 9 | 9 |
| Female Patients | 10 | | 7 | 7.5 |
| Spouse | 7 | | 4 | 4.5 |

**Table 4.25**
*Power — questions*

| Person | Session | | | |
|--------|---|---|---|---|
| | 1 | 2 | 3 | 4 |
| Couples | 18 | 23 | 19 | 16 |
| Male Patients | 16 | | 12 | 12 |
| Spouse | 15 | | 21 | 10 |
| Female Patients | 21 | | 18 | 22 |
| Spouse | 21 | | 21 | 18 |

**Table 4.26**
*Eye-gaze*

| Person | Session | | | |
|---|---|---|---|---|
| | 1 | 2 | 3 | 4 |
| Couples | 29 | 33 | 21 | 33 |
| Male Patients | 52 | | 38 | 47 |
| Spouse | 54 | | 62 | 67 |
| Female Patients | 62 | | 52 | 63 |
| Spouse | 49 | | 43 | 57 |

depressed couples use more control attempts than the surgical couples, and that this strategy seems to be a function of the acute disturbance since it drops significantly by Session 3. But, in addition, it is the women who use this technique rather than the men and that this sex role difference is consistent across all conditions. Other data which we have not shown here also suggest that not only do the women try to interrupt more frequently, but that they also succeed proportionately more often than the men. We appear, then to have discovered here a control strategy which is intensified in the depressive situation and which is characteristically used by the married woman. The use of questioning as a control mechanism does not emerge so clearly. The most striking finding is the degree to which the wives of depressed patients move into a complementary questionings mode which is quite unlike their style in the acute treatment phase or the pattern shown by their surgical counterparts. It is also different from anything shown by the depressed wives and their husbands. This is difficult to interpret, but it is thrown into relief if we compare the use of questions by the stranger and the depressed patient. The overall mean index figures here are 11 for the patient group and 35 for the stranger group, suggesting that the stranger is using this mode of communication to facilitate the interaction — and thus to control it. Perhaps the wives of the depressed patients are using the same technique in order to bring about the same effect.

Our final remarks on the power indices relate to the observations of eye-gaze. These data are most surprising because they show quite the reverse pattern from that which was expected. At the recovery session, gaze was significantly less than both the 'depressed' session and also the surgical session. We had anticipated that as in our earlier study, we would demonstrate reduced looking for the depressed patient in Session 1, but this was not so. The need for increased looking in Session 1 may be another indicator of the increased anxiety being expressed about the relationship at this point in time. The sex-linked behaviour *does* emerge strongly and the men in general use eye-gaze much less than the women. If we ignore patient status and simply compare men with women in all four sessions, then the women 'look' significantly more than the men in all sessions except the first one. This fits in with the expected pattern of looking for men and women. It suggests that depressed men and women look more when they are involved in a psychologically disturbed relationship than at other times. Therefore differences in gaze do seem to be influenced by a disturbance of mood, but gender differences continue to play an important part.

There is no straightforward way in which this pattern of results in the power domain can be simply understood. Certainly a simple model of enhanced dependency by the depressed spouse does not fit with the data we collected, since a number of measures show that the differences between the surgical and depressed couples increased with recovery rather than decreased. If anything, the depressed patients also increased their attempts at control in the acute hospitalization stage as well, so that in this situation there appears to be a power conflict. This is supported by our observations of the way in which gaze is used since here, too, the expected did not occur, which is more evidence that the notion of the dejected, powerless, and subordinate spouse needs revising. What we did discover was a powerful sex-linked pattern of the women trying to exercise control by their use of interruptions which is enhanced when the women are either depressed themselves, or their spouses are depressed. Finally we observed (once more) the very marked change in the communicative pattern which takes place when the stranger is introduced.

## Some Tentative Conclusions

This completes the presentation of the main data which we collected in our study of the couples, and now the reader needs something of a more synoptic view to draw the results and the ensuing discussion together. But it may well be that there appears to be a whole piece missing in the form of the substantive dialogues between the couples. This is to say that the process of communication which we present here was 'about' something and yet that does not figure in our data at all. But then the substantive discussion was not the focus of the study as it was designed and, indeed, would be very difficult to represent here without the aid of the actual recordings. Our task, rather, was to listen to the music of the communication rather than the words in order to see the kind of structure which lay behind the verbal messages of the couples. The first conclusion which occurs through the whole study is the responsive nature of the depressed patient's communication. In every domain which we studied and for male and female alike there were marked differences in the interaction between the two spouses and between the patient and stranger. This supports the recent field studies which begin to show the same kinds of phenomena as between clinical interaction patterns and family interaction patterns, but here the change is more abrupt since it occurs in the same setting as the first recording session. In earlier chapters we discussed the way in which some patterns of depressed behaviour were created and sustained by the couple so that the internal world of the patient and the interpersonal world of the couple become fused together into a system governed by what we called in Chapter 1 the depressive rule. What we saw between spouse and stranger was interaction free of this system constraint.

Next, we observed many intracouple differences when we compared the male/

female and the female/male marriages separately. An especially important shift was that which occurred for the depressed husbands into more affect-laden communication when they were acutely disturbed, but which reverted to a 'normal' pattern by recovery. The patient wives showed the intensification of negative affect but did not show the reverse pattern on recovery. Two complementary explanations may account for this, one of which is that in the depressed pattern, men more easily become regressively dependent, to which their wives respond by adopting a complementary nurturing maternal role. Then, by recovery, the couple move back into a symmetrical interaction pattern with the wives apparently able to adapt back quite easily. The depressed women on the other hand take up a regressive passive—aggressive stance to which their husbands cannot respond with a nurturant role, and therefore the disturbed communication pattern is maintained. These differences may well be enhanced by the prior quality of the female patient marriages which seemed to be poorer than those of the men.

Finally in this chapter we are able to describe sharp differences in pattern of communication between the normal and abnormal couples. The surgical couples were characterised by the contrast between challenge and support in the way they interacted. They use tension release, humour, and support to maintain an open problem-centred communication. In contrast the depressed couples communication is negative and uneven, overly protective and so they often appear to be mutually afraid of the process. The implications of this are clear, and suggest that the depressive response may well need to be viewed therapeutically in the interactive framework which will be our concern in the next two chapters.

# 5

# THE TREATMENT OF DEPRESSION

From what has been written so far it will be clear that we see depression as a fairly complex situation in which both the sufferer and their spouse (or partner) are intimately involved. We take the view, therefore, that any simple medical formula for treatment is likely to be of only limited value unless it takes account of the psychosocial situation of the patient. Obviously a therapist (of whatever persuasion) can only bring about certain changes — particularly if the treatment is taking place in the community — but these limited changes may then bring about other changes which are not under his control. For example it is widely held that the milder episodes of depression are self-limiting, but it may well be that the individual recovers from a bout of depression because his intimate life changes in such a way that he no longer needs to be depressed. The whole tone of our discussion so far is that depression is profoundly interpersonal as well as intrapersonal and that the way in which the other people respond to the depressed person is as important as anything that an outside agent can do.

But these cases are of course not often seen in clinics or hospitals. It is inevitable that treatment regimes have been worked out on people for whom the curative processes of living have failed, and much of the authors' experience is with the most disordered of all, since these are the ones who are referred for specialist help, generally when simpler measures have not been successful. Yet in one way we are strenuously trying to reverse this procedure in this book. By insisting on the primacy of the interpersonal world of the patient and then using this in the treatment process, we are trying to become aware of and to use the therapeutic power of ordinary people to its greatest effect.

We are not alone in this endeavour and an interesting recent example of this more complex approach to clinical work with depressed patients and spouses is that of Greene and his associates (1976). These authors too make use of a Systems Theory approach in their work and describe their experience of the depressed marriage as being symbiotic in character (i.e. one in which the individuals depend on each other for their existence). In their clinical sample, some of whom were treated over some years, they found the marriages were unusually stable when compared with the general instability of marriages in the United States. They also make the intriguing observation that many of their 'well' spouses ask for termination of medication so that the other partner may become his 'own self again'. This observation should not surprise us because our studies in the last chapter show the very intimate way in which the couple in depression interact.

Treatment mostly begins with the depressed person himself. It is frequently possible, as one gets to know the depressed individual's history in great detail, to discover that as he first began to experience the discomfort of depression he took some steps to mitigate it. Since much of the discomfort is often experienced as a bodily sensation, many of the alleviating activities are directed to the body. For example, some patients report that they tried exercise by taking unaccustomed walks, or playing squash, or some other equally simple change in their normal routine. Others turned to such procedures as massages and sauna baths; while others would turn to some traditional method of altering the way in which their body felt by taking patent medicines. The most common self-medications in this situations are either alcohol or purgatives, and the use of alcohol is not restricted to the person who becomes the patient but was quite frequently used as treatment by the spouse as well!

For other people the feeling of discomfort was associated with some problem with their every day situation. This may be in the form of dissatisfaction or staleness with their every day employment or with the home in which they live. It is not uncommon to find in the early stages of depression that the person who is identified as the patient, has sought to effect some major change in his daily way of life. Changes of job for a man or the finding of outside employment for the first time for the housewife are common. Similarly, major changes in the family situation are attempted by moving house.

Others seem to recognize at an early stage that their feelings of discomfort need some kind of intervention from outside themselves and they look for someone with whom they can talk about the way they feel. The identity of the outside helper varies enormously from social class to social class and from country to country. There is in most situations the 'approved' person to whom others in the community turn when in difficulties. People like the hairdresser and the barmaid play an important role here or, more formally, the telephone counselling agencies and clergymen are used in this way.

One of the main agencies which undertakes the treatment of a great number of individuals and couples who are depressed, is the Church. There are two main reasons why the Church should be involved in the treatment of depression. The first is that traditionally the Church has been the community which has cared for its individual members and, hence, has had a tradition of attempting to seek out those who have, for whatever reason, dropped out of the fellowship of the group. As depression is a very potent reason for individuals and couples to withdraw from the regular involvement in some kind of social activity like Church attendance, so the Church which is functioning effectively is likely to have made attempts to care for the couple with depression. The second reason is that those with depression frequently have an acute sense of guilt, unworthiness, hopelessness and lack of purpose. In so far as an individual will believe himself to be guilty, particularly if his everyday way of thinking includes a religious dimension, then he may well turn to the Church to find some relief from his sense of guilt. O. Hobart Mowrer (1961) has drawn attention to the role of guilt in many of the people who had consulted him for help with their depression. He points out, however, that in the majority of instances, the guilt was associated with some real failure or selfish action and, therefore, although the guilt was pathological in the sense of being disabling, it had got some basis in reality. His method of treatment included encouragement to the depressed person to seek for some reconciliation with the person who he felt he had wronged and an encouragement to make some kind of reparation for the guilt-causing act.

Some people do try to use their spouses or partners to get things right again but this does not always work out well. The problem is that kindly reassurance is not accepted because the depressed person simply cannot believe what his spouse says about him. This rejection of help which has been sought then seems to invalidate the partner as a helper and this rejection process becomes itself part of the depressive system. The difficulty is that the depressed system may become a closed one which is self-validating and one that therefore cannot be changed from inside. This is often closely related to barely-concealed conflict which neither partner may acknowledge because they fear the potential destruction which they think they perceive.

If these efforts at self-help (at whatever level) fail, then the individual or family hopefully seeks further help. From the point of view of the professional sitting in his office consulting with those who come to him, it is easy to disregard the attempts which a person or couple have taken to mitigate the effects of the depression and to regard the depression as having an inevitability about it which nullifies the homespun treatment attempt. However, what we do not know is the degree of the success which attends these efforts by others who are *not* unduly handicapped by the early stages of depression, and who appear to make a recovery without recourse to the professional. It certainly seems on reflection that the lives of one's friends and neighbours indicate that such attempts to treat depression are not infrequently effective without recourse to any other agency.

## The Medical Process

As we turn to talk about the medical forms of treatment for depression it is worth reminding ourselves that those who actually get into the medical caring net, form only a small proportion of those who can be regarded as suffering from depression. Both the English study of Watts (1966), and the American study of Srole and coworkers (1962), indicate that probably only about one in twenty of those who could be regarded as depressed find their way into formal medical treatment. Watts (1966) talks about the 'iceberg of depression'. In his rural general practice he estimated that about one hundred and fifty of every thousand of the population which he served would have, what he called, subclinical depressive features. In any one year he, as a general practitioner, would see about sixteen new cases, of these about two would be referred to a psychiatrist, less than one for mental hospital admission and .1 per thousand of population at risk would commit suicide each year. In his study of South London women, Brown (1975) found that 15% of his control sample were psychiatrically disturbed and a further 10% had minor psychiatric symptoms. These figures emphasize the importance of the non-medical forms of treatment for depression. It is certain that as far as Great Britain is concerned, the majority of medical treatment of depression occurs within general practice.

Once the couple enter the medical system a new phase of treatment has commenced. The first stage of the treatment is the initial exploratory history-taking interview during which it becomes possible for the interviewer to gain a clear understanding of the processes which are involved, the depth of distress and also to decide on the most effective way of proceeding with treatment. At the end of the first interview which in the general situation may be relatively brief, but which in the hospital clinic may take much longer, it is usual for the person who is being consulted to indicate clearly how he sees and thinks about the problem which the couple present. It is not uncommon in this situation for the couple to express the relief which they feel that someone has been able to understand and see clearly the possibilities for treatment of the condition with which they have presented. For the couple, whether they have been seen individually or together, the spelling out of the details of their problem often brings it into focus in a way which they have been unable to achieve by themselves. In this new perspective lie the possibilities for further successful treatment.

Before we proceed to a further discussion of the medical treatment of correctly identified depression, it is important to acknowledge that some depressed patients are misidentified and treated other than by appropriate methods. Because many of the symptoms of depression are concentrated in the body, either in the form of pains or discomforts, this leads the physician to investigate the individual with a view to determining whether or not there is some underlying pathology in the area of the body of which the patient is complaining. In one sense, of course, this *is* a form of treatment since the patient has embarked upon a series of investigations, and this is particularly so if those who are conducting the investigations are caring and concerned for the person involved. However, persistent symptoms, particularly associated with weight loss, which may well occur with depression, can lead to extensive investigations including investigative surgery.

This misidentification of the problem points up one very real difficulty which exists for a couple who have the problem of depression. The more the patient and spouse begin to think of their problem as one which is 'medical' the more there is a tendency to think of the problem as being isolated or contained within the partner who has become identified as the patient. This encourages the patient to adopt the well recognized patient role whereas the spouse is regarded as the unaffected or fit partner. In this they are separated and instead of having roles which in other situations are reciprocal, the roles are now altered so that one is dependent, the other is supportive and caring. The deliberate use of this shift in roles may form part of the treatment and some workers, e.g. Greene and coworkers (1976), use this possible change in, and recognition of, roles in an attempt to gain some therapeutic purchase on the problem. Having identified the patient, they then collaborate with the spouse to develop the therapeutic potential of the spouse by agreeing that with certain types of depression, the depression resides in the patient because of factors of inheritance and of abnormal biochemistry. This they believe does a number of things, including removing any sense of responsibility or fault from the spouse and from the patient, and also puts the problem into a category which can largely be tackled by exhibiting various kinds of physical therapeutic procedures. It is clear that any of the traditional treatments of depression, whether they be of the drug variety, electro-convulsive therapy or even admission to hospital for the patient, can all be seen as more clearly identifying the patient in the sick role and distinguishing very clearly between the sick and the well partners in the marriage.

In our discussion below of the treatment of depression, we will review the various forms of treatment which are available and discuss them in terms of how they seem to influence the problem of depression in the setting of the marriage. It was evident from our studies of hospitalized patients and their spouses that there are a number of changes in the interaction which occur during the course of treatment. At the end of the treatment time when the problem appears to be resolved, both the patient and the spouse were found to be different. It should also be clear that in subsequent discussion much of what we have to say applies as much to the physician working in the general practice situation as to the specialist working in the hospital clinic.

### Physical Treatment

Once the problem has been identified the most common form of treatment, particularly in the general practice situation, is the use of antidepressant drugs. These drugs have been used enthusiastically now for a number of years, although the enthusiasm often outstrips the scientific evidence in favour of their validity as treatments for depression. The fact that the title 'antidepressant' has become so firmly established attests as much to the need for some form of treatment as it does to their supposed efficacy. Without any doubt, the drugs which are in every day use as part of the treatment of depression, whichever of the three pharmacological categories they belong to, all have significant pharmacological effects. It is certain that each of these drugs in its own way alters the way in which the individual perceives himself. Most of them have a fairly significant effect in reducing the level of distress for the individual. Some psychotherapists view drugs as influencing the therapeutic process negatively by (a) casting the patient into the medical role and (b) by influencing their capacity to feel appropriately about the psychodynamic processes under analysis. Others view drugs as contributing positively by reducing anxiety levels and feelings of guilt to a level where they become more accessible to psychotherapeutic intervention. However, it is fairly clear that all the drugs in this category have some significant side-effects and do not return the person per se to normal. We have noted above how Greene and coworkers (1976), reported that some of their spouses wanted the medication withdrawn so that the patient could be returned to normal. Mayer (1975) has considerably extended this discussion and reports her conclusions that antidepressant drugs often leave people feeling in themselves unusual and their spouses perceiving the patient as abnormal. Our own practice has confirmed that it is not unusual for patients to report that they did not feel well until they had stopped taking their antidepressant medication.

A good example of this phenomena was recently observed in a 50-year old physician who became acutely depressed and who had been taking antidepressants for a number of months. His treatment included conjoint psychotherapy for the whole of the period of the depression and at one stage he was treated briefly with E.C.T. When he had returned to work and had begun to function well again in the setting of his marriage and family, he still had a number of symptoms which had persisted for the whole of the course of the depression. These symptoms included feelings of heaviness, difficulty in getting started in the morning and a feeling that there was a lack of point in life with no sense of enjoyment of every day things. Within a few days of cessation of the tricyclic antidepressants, this physician and his spouse reported on the marked change in his demeanour. He, himself, reported on the way in which he now felt different and free from his previous symptoms.

Whatever may be the pharmacological effect of the antidepressant drugs on the central nervous system, as far as the marriage is concerned, there are a number of therapeutically important effects which can be observed. The relationship between taking the medication and the various psychological processes, in particular the interactional processes, is complex and has yet to be unravelled in any great detail. In addition to the changes in the internal environment in the patient which occurs as a result of the medication, there are also those changes which stem from the expectations of the couple with regard to the treatment itself.

When there is a satisfactory response to the antidepressant medication, one of the first things which is reported by the couple is a decrease in their level of discomfort. This is talked about in such terms as there being less tension or that life seems easier in some way. Sometimes it is possible to discern that instead of the tense rather rigid formal way in which the couple articulate together, there is a new kind of freedom in their interaction.

Perhaps the most striking change which can be seen is the way in which the couple now talk very much more freely with each other. Enquiries will often reveal that this freedom in talking extends beyond the consulting room into their every day life, and that subjects which were once taboo or unduly painful, can now be raised again between them and faced in a way which has a different quality and character. It is as if the couple has been able to move beyond the stereotyped repetitive and unproductive exchanges which characterized their previous interaction to the stage beyond this in which both felt that there was a measure of satisfaction in their relationship. This observation may well be the corollary to the methods of treatment which have been devised by behavioural therapists and which we will discuss in more detail below.

No discussion of the use of antidepressants would be complete without some comment on the problem which exists in those marriages in which suicide of the patient is a real possibility and which Ayd (1961) found was about 30% of a large sample of depressed patients. In suicide we see the extreme of the breakdown in the caring and sustaining bonds within the marriage, and one is often left with the distinct impression that the spouse has in many ways facilitated the suicide or the suicide attempt. One of the striking and disturbing features of the literature (Morgan and coworkers, 1975) is the very high number of people attempting to kill themselves or to harm themselves, who use antidepressant drugs for this purpose.

One of the mechanisms which seems to be involved is that in those marriages where suicide or suicide attempt occurs, the beginning of treatment with antidepressants has been the signal for the spouse to change his behaviour in a significant way. These changes almost invariably are in the direction of detachment and withdrawal in the marriage so that the patient is left more isolated and less supported. Rather than the good and healing processes which we have discussed above coming into operation, the reverse seems to occur so that the psychological options for the patient are reduced rather than enhanced.

Perhaps one of the most significant features of those marriages in which a suicide attempt occurs is the way in which the spouse largely refuses any discussion of the suicide risk which may exist, and will leave large amounts of medication readily available to the patient. That this behaviour is not the fruit of ignorance is illustrated in a recent case. A physician's wife who was severely depressed was given antidepressant medication at the beginning of treatment. The physician was well versed in the dangers of the medication and of the possibility that suicide was a real risk. Notwithstanding this knowledge (and a discussion with the psychiatrist who was caring for the couple) towards the end of her existing week's supply of drugs he prescribed a fortnight's supply of medication for his wife, justifying the action on the grounds that he did not want her to run out of medication over the weekend. She thus had access to two or three days' supply plus the medication which was prescribed by her husband. He gave all the tablets into her care and then proceeded to spend more than the usual amount of time at his place of work. While he was away she took the whole of the medication which was available to her.

The very real possibility of suicide is one of the factors in severely depressed individuals which may well indicate the use of E.C.T. as treatment. Despite widespread use of this method, there is still considerable controversy about the rationale of its effect and indications for its use. It is most frequently used therapeutically when the person becomes quite inaccessible to other approaches because of complete withdrawal, pervasive and compelling thoughts (especially of death), or extremely agitated behaviour. The pros and cons of E.C.T. are well summarized by Clare (1976), but many of the comments which were made with regard to antidepressant drugs also apply to E.C.T:, particularly in the setting of the marriage. Because of the dramatic and often mysterious aspects of the treatment, together with admission to hospital, the focus of the treatment is even more clearly seen to be the patient. These features can combine together to make it even less likely that the spouse will feel involved or connected with the treatment. The fact that we know so little about the way in which E.C.T. has an effect on the internal environment of the patient and produces the therapeutic changes, may only enhance the feeling of the spouse that mysterious things are occurring of which they have very little part.

Admission to hospital is a very important step in the treatment of depression. Most authorities regard this as being indicated when there is a danger of an individual harming himself or where the necessity for physical treatment becomes imperative and cannot be adequately administered on an outpatient basis. From the point of view of our present discussion, there are a number of important points to make about the therapeutic value of admission to hospital. In the majority of instances, the person who is admitted is the partner with the most obvious symptoms but very occasionally admission of both partners can be a highly successful therapeutic strategy.

Frequently after admission the individual will report that the procedure of being admitted has been helpful and that they feel some lessening in the intensity of their symptoms when they are in hospital. It is not uncommon for a patient to be admitted to hospital and to receive no further change in treatment other than to spend their time by being involved in the hospital routine, and yet after a period of days or at most a few weeks, to make a good clinical recovery from their depression. It is clear from this observation that admission to hospital, and the hospital environment itself, are very important treatment modalities which also affect the family.

As far as the marriage is concerned the first thing that happens on admission is that there is a geographical separation of the patient and spouse. For a while, most of their lives are lived in a different situation, and they are prevented from the close intimate interaction which had characterized their relationship prior to the admission. This separation can be used in a very positive way in that it enables each of the partners to have enough distance from the other in order to begin to see the relationship and their lives without the constraints which are normally imposed on them by their lives. This can be regarded as 'time out' and may well be a necessary phase in the treatment.

Admission is also useful in that it can indicate quite clearly to the partner and to other people in society, that there is one member of the partnership who is for a while grossly disadvantaged by the depression, and this can be used in a positive and therapeutic way. Expectations for someone who is sick and who is in hospital are entirely different from those which obtain when the same person is living in the normal home situation. This kind of process can only continue for a relatively short time otherwise it is likely to become destructive rather than helpful.

The comments which have been made above in relationship to hospital admission as a form of treatment for depression, could easily be interpreted in terms which focus on the individual psychology of the partners rather than on the nature and quality of their interaction. To remove responsibilities and to decrease pressure seem to focus on the individual behaviour of the partners rather than on the marriage itself.

So that we may formulate more accurately the essential features of the therapeutic process, it is important to use the General Systems Theory model in order to encompass what happens in this kind of situation more completely. The traditional family or marriage system is necessarily disrupted by admission to hospital. For a while, at least, the marriage as it existed up to the time of admission is no longer the marriage in which the partners are involved. In this sense they now have some distance from their accustomed behaviour and, therefore, are able perhaps for the first time to be able to see the processes involved in the depression and begin to rehearse strategies for changing in anticipation of re-entering the intimacy of marriage again.

As has been observed by Watzlawick and coworkers (1967; 1974), it is almost impossible to understand the system in which one lives and is involved and it is difficult to do very much about changing the system while the involvement is preoccupying most of one's time. Hence, to step for a while outside the system gives an opportunity to see it again more clearly and begin to formulate therapeutic changes.

## Psychological Treatment

We have stressed all the way through that we see the depression in terms of the nature and quality of the interaction which surrounds the person who is labelled as the patient. We have argued that because of the complexity of the interaction which exists in the social network, and in particular in marriage, that the treatment only makes sense when it is associated with changes in the interaction. We believe that, despite the complexity of the factors involved in an interaction, we can discern some of the important aspects of psychotherapy which have a purchase in the depressive situation. We have noted above the very real difficulties which exist in talking about an interaction and we have cited our own research to show that even though the complexity is only slightly lessened as a result of our efforts it is possible to talk about important aspects of the interaction, and we believe that these are of real relevance to the processes which occur in psychotherapy. Our own work showed that the traditional ways of thinking about depression do not contain the richness of description which depression warrants.

We would, therefore, argue that any psychotherapy which wishes to use the information which is now available in a therapeutic way must begin to move away from the traditional description. Perhaps the most important observation is that the spouse of the depressed patient undergoes a series of important changes during the course of the disorder. We will look at therapeutic intervention with the couple rather than the individual in our next chapter.

As opposed to a couple who are without depression, the depressed couple demonstrate a preoccupation with themselves, leading at times to an almost total exclusion of people and events outside their own marriage. This has some significance particularly for the relatively inexperienced psychotherapists who may see in this preoccupation not a symptom of the disorder but rather a characteristic style of interaction which may lead the therapist to use a pejorative description for the marriage. This kind of response by the therapist could provide a real hurdle to effecting useful changes in the interaction.

For many years, indeed for centuries, it has been noticed that depressed individuals seem to respond far less readily and quickly to stimuli from others. We have been able to demonstrate that this responsiveness is not just a characteristic of the individual depressed person but rather is a characteristic of both partners in the marriage. This, we believe, has real significance for the psychotherapeutic efforts which are made with a depressed couple.

We have also been able to demonstrate that the observations which may be made of the individuals in the marriage when they are seen individually are quite different from the kinds of observations which can be made when the couple is seen together

The characteristic features which are conventionally used to assess the severity of depression are seen with far greater clarity at this time. Yet despite what has just been said about the responsiveness of the partners to each other, it is also clear from our studies that one of the characteristics of the communicational patterns which exists in depressed marriages is that the partners may engage in a very high level of disruption of each others messages. This seems to be an indication of the level of distress in the relationship. The importance to psychotherapy, particularly if the couple are being seen together, is fairly obvious because any intervention by the therapist can be disrupted in the same way as the couple disrupt each others messages. This is disconcerting for the therapist, certainly until he recognizes that this is part of the process which occurs in depression.

For a number of reasons it often seems quite appropriate to see the individual partners rather than to see the couple together. This enables the exploration of issues which cannot be readily explored in the conjoint situation. It also enables the individual to build up a relationship with the therapist which, itself, can have some therapeutic purchase on the depressive process. It has been our experience with some couples that although the partner has been available, it has been more appropriate to work principally with the patient partner and to limit contact with the spouse. This situation obtains where personality difficulties predominate for one individual or where it is clear that the couple do not wish to change the equilibrium which they have established between themselves. It may be that there is a strong drive to keep the marriage stable but little commitment to improving the quality or level of intimacy of the relationship. In other words, the couple have covertly agreed upon the distance they intend to maintain between themselves and do not welcome any intervention which challenges this. An external event may have made this arrangement more fragile and depressive symptoms emerged in one partner. However, individual therapy to assist the depressed partner to clarify his/her position in the relationship together with separate interviews for the spouse may be more in keeping with their needs.

We can illustrate this type of problem in the case of a dental mechanic and his wife who had sustained a distant but workable relationship over a number of years and during that time had adopted three children. More recently the wife had had a hysterectomy and had become depressed post-operatively and developed very hostile feelings for her husband who had not offered her the support and help she had anticipated. She had withdrawn sexually and he had become hypercritical of her, expressing her feeling that she was totally inadequate as a mother. They were both concerned to keep the marriage going, partly for the sake of the children, and also because of their ambivalent feelings for each other. The wife responded to antidepressants in the first instance and found individual psychotherapy very helpful in understanding her resentments and her need to be punitive to her husband. She was able to let go of her tensions and anxieties and accept the nature of the relationship she had established over the years. Her husband was prepared to come to isolated interviews but fought shy of any greater involvement, prefering his wife to be the patient.

We have also discovered, what has been observed by other people, notably

McLean (1976), that it is not always possible to involve the spouse in the treatment of the depressed person. There are many reasons why this appears to be so but most importantly it seems to turn on the belief that 'the depression of my wife or husband is nothing to do with me other than being an inconvenience'. The traditional medical view of treatment of depression, of course, fosters this attitude and at times makes it impossible to incorporate the spouse in the kind of treatment which we would advocate. McLean reports that in his experience, it is almost invariably the husbands who are difficult to involve in treatment, whereas he finds the wives of depressed men very much more easily incorporated in the treatment programme. Therefore for practical reasons it can be difficult to work with the couple and one's therapeutic thrust must then be confined to the one labelled as the patient.

The ongoing issues within the relationship are frequently very difficult to talk about, either because the patient lacks sufficient understanding or insight to conceptualize the problems or lacks the necessary verbal fluency to deal with the therapeutic ideas which the therapist is suggesting. One way of handling this difficulty is for the therapist to provide the language and to teach the patients the appropriateness of it. One good example of this is seen in Transactional Analysis. In this particular form of psychotherapy the notion of roles plays a very important part. Transactional Analysis provides a simple structure which can assist the patient and spouse in understanding their present behaviour in both personal and interactional terms. It also gives them an awareness of the personal responsibility they can exhibit in effecting behaviour change. Thus the couple have an opportunity of stepping back from the immediate situation and viewing it more objectively.

The use of the 'roles' language in the therapeutic situation becomes valuable in a therapeutic sense when the therapist has what Truax and Carhuff (1967) call accurate empathy. For example, there is no value in talking about a parent/child relationship existing in the marriage unless the patient can see and feel that the description is appropriate. The purpose of introducing the role consideration into the treatment is not an end in itself, and unless it becomes the basic for which changes in behaviour can be made, it may well become a diversionary activity which delays the hoped for therapeutic result.

It is important to rehearse what was made clear in Chapter 2, that in the therapeutic situation roles are not static. The other important aspects of roles are that they are not mutually exclusive of other roles. That is to say, that if an individual appears to be fulfilling one particular role as a father, vis-à-vis his wife, he may also at the same time be behaving in the role of the seductive lover. Despite these comments it is frequently possible to see clearly the predominant roles that are played by each of the partners, and the way in which these roles have changed with time and, we believe, with treatment.

One of the interesting questions which is frequently raised during treatment with psychotherapy is: 'What provides the motive for change in behaviour and experience after there has been intellectual understanding of the particular situation in which the pathology exists?'. Watzalawick and coworkers (1974) discussed this issue at some length, and point to the way in which the formulation of a problem and, in particular, the way in which the problem can be categorized can frequently provide the situation for a change in behaviour. It would seem that the utilization of the 'roles' notion for analysing the problems within marriages, can indeed provide that kind of situation which allows changes to take place. However simply providing the opportunity which permits changes to take place does not answer the query we raised above. In fact, it is unlikely that there is an adequate explanation available which can be expressed in behavioural terms and we are often cast back on an explanation which includes such notions as 'trust' and 'commitment'. Neither of these terms allow an adequate behavioural description although they do seem to meet the experience which we share with both individuals and couples during treatment.

In the last few years there have been a series of attempts to introduce more strictly behavioural forms of treatment for those who are depressed. Although many of these seem to focus very much on the individual as the patient, there have been some attempts to include the spouse in these forms of treatment. Those who have applied the behavioural therapy approaches to depression, talk in terms of the way in which there is a low rate of 'response contingent positive reinforcement' of behaviour in depression. Treatment efforts are directed towards there being a change from negative feedback to a much more positive form of feedback. Much of this treatment is framed in communicational terms and strategies are devised so that instead of the negative reinforcement which is the characteristic lot of the depressive, he is reinforced positively by those round about him. This can have a direct application within the setting of marriage, particularly if the spouse is regarded as the provider of the appropriate kind of stimuli and reinforcement. McLean and coworkers (1973) make the interesting observation that too much negative feedback has the effect of criticism which is destructive or the individual's view of himself and confirms him in his depressive experience, while too much positive feedback results in the loss of credibility of the person who is providing this reinforcement; this observation links up with the comment which was made above in terms of 'trust' and 'commitment' Both of which concepts are difficult to sustain in a setting which lacks sincerity or in which the integrity of the other person is in doubt.

Costello (1972) has written about the complexity of the treatment situation when using behavioural methods. He points out that it is not just a simple matter of providing the right kind of stimulus and the appropriate reinforcement for the positive behaviour which is desired. He emphasizes that the stimulus and reinforcement, in order to be effective, must be tailor-made to the recipient. The depressive processes as far as the recipient is concerned, are certainly going to influence the way in which he will receive the various communicational stimuli as they impinge on him. For example, a simple sentence like 'You are only moderately depressed' may be interpreted by a person who is viewing the whole of life in a depressive way, quite differently from the way in which it was intended. It may be that the patient would see the 'moderate' word as indicating that he could still continue to get worse rather than being in a particular state which the observer judges to be in the 'not severe' category.

Before we conclude this chapter it will probably be helpful to give the reader the outline of a particularly complex case in which various kinds of treatment procedures — both informal and formal — were involved. This will illustrate the complex nature of many chronic cases of depression in which the disorder and the treatment appear very frequently to become intertwined into a totally confusing knot. The couple concerned were in their late forties when they were finally referred to us for advice and treatment. The referral was apparently for their marital problems, but their battle with depression soon came to light.

The husband was a moderately successful design engineer with a large firm who also had a small private income from his long-dead father. His wife had never worked outside the home and the couple had four children. Their difficulties started ten years previously when the wife's mother (to whom she was devoted) died very suddenly and tragically from a brain tumour. She was desolated by this death and nothing that family or friends could do was of much avail. Her husband, too, was strangely affected by the mother-in-law's demise and his work began to suffer. He eventually decided that the solution would be to move from the town in which they were living and to start again elsewhere. His wife was totally opposed to this but, in describing this decision, he said that she was morbidly preoccupied with the place and not at that time able to make a judgement. Just before the move (and about ten months after her mother's death), a new G.P. in their practice prescribed for the wife some antidepressant medication which had a remarkable effect on her and she became much improved — although still totally opposed to the move.

Nevertheless they did move, but her husband at this time made most of the decisions, even finally deciding on their new house because she was 'so indecisive'. For a time things were reasonable and the wife recovered from her acute depressive feelings. Then the husband's work (which was much less satisfactory than his previous job) began to go badly. Whether this was his work situation or his capacity remained unclear. Eventually he became acutely depressed and stopped working. His wife at this time became very caring and got him to see, first their G.P., and then subsequently a psychiatrist. He too, was prescribed an antidepressant drug and had brief clinic follow-up visits. Having taken the drug for about six months, and gained some relief from unpleasant somatic symptoms, he one day decided to seek (and found) a job change in the same town. From then on he improved progressively. For a time things appeared to be adjusted, albeit precariously, but then the wife had a hysterectomy at the age of 46. Following this she once again became depressed and after a few months began to be treated with antidepressant drugs. This time she did not stop taking them because the relationship between husband and wife became increasingly difficult. She became more demanding in many areas — financially, socially, and sexually — and he became more and more truculent and withdrawn. Eventually he left home for some days but was so shocked at his behaviour that he persuaded his wife to seek help with him.

In this case we slowly withdrew the wife's medication and began to work conjointly with them on the traumatic events of the previous decade. At each occasion it transpired that they had never 'dared' to talk about their real responses to the situation and each other because of their mutual fear of the aggression which (they supposed) might destroy them. They had in fact almost taken over the roles of rivalrous brother and sister with each other and used a number of sessions with the therapist to work this problem out. The husband's hitherto unspoken attachment to his wife's mother also emerged — as did her anger about this.

Occasionally the wife would feel acutely suicidal in the context of the discussion of some of these painful issues between them, but slowly they were able to take up their adult relationship where they left off over ten years before. Active therapy continued over six months of weekly sessions and was concluded when they decided to set up in a small retail business on their own — something which both had actually long wanted to do. As the reader can see, there were social, medical, and psychological changes which this couple tried as they worked with their problems. They were both intelligent and sensitive people, but lacked a helper who could apparently take a broad view of their mutual depression. Undoubtedly the medication helped for a time, but then the original problem broke through again, and possibly in the future a joint therapy regime may still be necessary.

## Conclusion

Since the introduction of the effective physical forms of therapy for depression forty-odd years ago, very large numbers of people have benefited by formal psychiatric treatment. There are also large numbers of people who have benefited from various forms of psychotherapy and in the last few years it has been possible to establish a rationale for the use of combined physical and psychotherapeutic methods of treatment for the benefit of patients. We believe that by considering depression within the setting of marriage, it is possible to extend in a very powerful way the intervention of professional mental health workers in the treatment of those who are depressed.

We further believe that evidence is now rapidly accumulating which lends support to our view, and we are hopeful that there will be continuing changes in this area, particularly in relation to the way in which there is a rehumanization of the philosophy which underlies much of the practice. We are concerned to move away from the reductionist forms of philosophy which have been behind the organic forms of treatment and the severely psychoanalytic psychotherapies. By espousing a non-reductionistic view of treatment we are able to embark upon the kind of treatments which we have discussed above. We have found that our treatment, whether it be in the emergency crisis intervention-type of situation, or whether it be in the more formal outpatient situation with the treatment spreading over perhaps a number of months, has in both places found confirmation and support. The next chapter will develop this particular therapeutic approach in greater detail.

# 6

# MARITAL THERAPY AND DEPRESSION

In the previous chapter we discussed the general issues which arise on therapeutic intervention with depressed people. Our discussion ranged over various treatment regimes, but was particularly concerned with the interpersonal effects of the actual request for treatment and the approaches which the clinician must make to the important people in the patient's life. We also examined in that chapter the important place which some types of organic treatment may have in the treatment process. All writers who approach the complex phenomena of depression agree with the fact that the vegetative functions as Beck (1967) called them may be very involved in the disorder so that the problem often appears heavily somatised. But we have discussed in Chapter 1 the logical objections to considering this as *the* basis for the understanding for the vast number of depressive disorders. Transient periods of depression may appear in a number of psychological disturbance patterns, but the therapeutic approach which we wish to consider here is for those people in which the pattern of disturbance is sufficiently sustained for the diagnosis to be primarily that of depression.

At first sight it may appear paradoxical to suggest that the abject, tearful, intensely self-centred morbid person sitting in the general practitioner's waiting room or the psychiatric out-patient clinic should be helped by an *inter* rather than a *intra*personal therapeutic method. It may appear that they are not even aware of the people with whom they live, let alone capable of interacting with them. This is of course a very familiar argument against any interpersonal approach for any psychological disturbance and once more relates to the type of general theory of human behaviour with which the clinician may be working.

In fact, a simple appreciation of the clinical situation shows that the situation itself is obviously interpersonal, and that the evaluation of the severity of the person's depression will rest as much upon the emotional impact which the patient makes on the clinician as on the symptomatic discomfort which the person reports about himself. This does require what Kuhn (1962) has called in another more cerebral context a paradigm shift in order to be able to think in an interpersonal therapeutic context, but we have also already provided the reader with experimental evidence from our own studies that the depressed person is far from uncommunicative.

Chapter 4 outlines some of the ways in which the patterns of communication between spouses differs significantly as between the depressed and the non-depressed patients, but there was no suggestion that the depressed patients were *unable* to communicate with their spouses.

The view that much of the disturbance may be interpersonal is fortunately not ours alone. We have already referred to recent studies which have used this set of ideas of which the two most important are those by Weissman and Paykel (1974), and Brown, Bhrolchain and Harris (1975). It is important to identify here a very large gap in our knowledge at the present time which is that both of these studies are of women and that at the present time there is no similar study of depressed men other than our own. What our studies have shown is that the interpersonal style and thus the problems of the depressed male couple are sharply different from those of the female couple, and we will discuss this later in the chapter. It appears that there is a widely prevalent stereotype of the depressed women as caught in many social conflicts peculiar to this stage of our cultural development. The male appears largely to escape from these pathological processes which seem to make their presence felt primarily among women. The prevalence rates for depression are generally accepted from the evidence as in a ratio of 2–2.5/1.0 (female/male). Weissman and Paykel in the introduction to their study speculate as to whether we are entering an 'age of melancholy' in the Western world and describe it as the 'Epidemic of the 70s'. They suggest that it is more acceptable for females to express depressive feelings and to seek psychiatric help than for males and note that the higher incidence of alcoholism in males might be a parallel disorder. However, since depression holds equal place with anxiety as the most common psychological symptom pattern there are obviously large numbers of men involved. (Shepherd and coworkers 1966). For the moment, however, we lack the detailed studies which would supplement those which we now have for women and it may well be that men have different expressive outlets for depressive feelings within our culture.

We will turn now to the study of Brown and his colleagues who describe depressive conditions as 'social phenomena'. They make their position clear in the beginning of their paper by writing (p. 227):

'...depressive conditions are not only common, but in large part the result of experiences that are strongly related to social position... In this paper we are particularly concerned with the aetiological role of certain kinds of adverse life events. But we show that much more is involved than the random occurrence of such events; for instance vulnerability is greatly increased by the presence of specific kinds of ongoing social circumstances.'

We have already discussed (Chapter 3) the detailed findings from his study, which demonstrated social class differences and clarified the vulnerability factors in terms of life events and social circumstances. Their most interesting finding in relation to the question of therapy was in the area of assessing the quality and quantity of the intimate relationships of these women.

They found that when the women were divided into those with an intimate confidante and those without such a person, the lack of that relationship increased the likelihood of depression about nine times. And these intimate relationships were almost entirely between the women concerned and a man — either husband or boyfriend. Many women had good relationships with women friends and relatives, but these were not 'close, intimate and confiding' in the words of the investigators.

This was also strongly related to social class so that the young working class wives were five times more vulnerable than their middle class sisters. In the older wives, however, the intimacy values for the working class women returned to similar levels to the middle class wives. We can speculate with Brown and colleagues about the protective value of a good intimate relationship in the face of stressful events and other vulnerability factors. They suggest that although the stressful events are impossible to control prospectively (and once they have happened are obviously beyond control), that nevertheless intimacy in relationships may be potentially influencable by psychotherapeutic methods. It may be that these couples need more support and understanding from resources within the community than we are able to supply in our modern urban style of living. Break up of communities, high rise flats and the anonymity of city life must all contribute to a reduction in the emotional support which smaller more well-defined communities can offer. The authors suggest that the more verbal middle class wife who has an adequate intimate relationship with her partner is more able and likely to seek help at times of stress.

It is interesting to consider how social class affects the interactive ingredients which go towards a good supportive intimate relationship. Communication occurs at two levels, the explicit or verbal and implicit or non-verbal. Verbal skills and sophistications clearly play an important role in clarifying the subtleties and details of the individual's experience. But in addition there must also be a confidence and a capacity to be explicit and make clear a deficiency or need, and risk the possible conflict which may ensue. In a middle class environment there is a greater emphasis on verbal fluency and self-expression, quite apart from the young adult's extended period of education and training. In general, girls show greater verbal fluency than boys although there is said to be a reverse difference in their reasoning capacity. It was certainly our experience amongst some of the working class couples in our study that we noted a flow of demanding language from the wives which was greeted by monosyllabic grunts and replies by their near inarticulate partners. They were not capable of dealing with their differences and negotiating a compromise through their use of words. However, at a non-verbal level the capacity to be perceptive and intuitive varies enormously at all levels of intelligence and attainment.

In general, the more expressive role of the female equips her to be sharper and more tuned in to the finer differences here. It may be that the vulnerable married working class mother lacks the verbal skills of her middle class sister and, although acutely aware of the deficiencies in her relationship, is misunderstood by her partner as a result of a diminished repertoire of resources for communication. The increased use of expressiveness both through choice of words and tone of voice was a feature of the depressed couples in our study, which supports our argument that the verbal mode is of key importance in successful communication.

The interactive difficulties in the depressed marriage were clarified in more detail by Weissman and Paykel in their study which included 40 depressed women and a matched control sample of 40 women living under similar circumstances in the community. There were, however, a disproportionate absolute number of working class women, although they formed identical proportions of each group and in this sense were matched. The two groups were compared with each other both at the commencement of treatment for the depressives and eight months later, and assessments were made both of depressive symptoms and social adjustment.

The women involved were between 25 and 60 and about three quarters of both samples were currently married. The initial observations of the depressed women suggested that they lacked both autonomy and intimacy in their marital relationships. Impaired communication was a major problem and was particularly poor when (to quote the authors) 'unspoken diffuse misery was conveyed to a spouse with the implication that it was either caused by or should be alleviated by him'. In addition the problem of hostile friction was a very real one. These investigators make the important point that in many cases the conventional psychodynamic wisdom about enabling the patient to show hostility is not necessary. Indeed, they suggest that it is more important to help the women to accept and control anger.

The treatment regimes which involved these patients were uniformly antidepressant drug therapy initially, and then a random allocation to either monthly supportive psychotherapy or more intense once or twice-weekly dyadic psychotherapy. Often within a month of commencing treatment the unpleasant physical symptoms had abated, but the interpersonal difficulties improved much more slowly. The psychotherapy regime was especially important in preventing relapse. But impaired communication and interpersonal friction remained a problem especially in the area of marital roles. It is actually surprising to find that despite their evidence the authors did *not* use any form of marital therapy.

Taken together these two detailed studies seem to demonstrate that marital systems operate in both positive and negative directions. That is, that where the spouses of women are supportive and close the depressive response may be cut short. But this may often be lacking and in these cases, the marital scene becomes a major source of continued tension and conflict, often with a marked incapacity for either spouse to be able to achieve any kind of change. This, then suggests that a therapeutic intervention at the level of the marital system will either strengthen an important resource for support and change, or else at least neutralize the interpersonal system from having very disabling effects.

## Models for Marital Therapy

We will now turn our attention to the range of models which have sprung up during the past decade or so. The historical perspective of marital therapy was well reviewed by Sager in 1966 and since then a proliferation of articles and descriptions have appeared mainly in the American literature. The striking exception to this is Dicks (1967) account of his pioneering work in this field at the Tavistock Clinic and the more recent review of Marital Therapy by Crown (1976). Two other more recent publications in this country by Skynner (1976) and Walrond-Skinner (1976) have been written in the more general family area with limited reference to marital work.

In a forthcoming review of the family and marital therapy field which is more wide-ranging than anything previously published Gurman and Kniskern (1977) have now located 200 relevant studies. Although they are very critical of the quality of many of these studies, they also comment that the general standard *is* moving in the right direction.

Unfortunately, too, it is an area of work in which therapeutic enthusiasm outruns the more difficult business of theoretical understanding, and the very much more difficult business of adequate research evaluation. So the present picture is one of sprawling therapeutic methods applied to a bewildering variety of problems in a very non-specific way and carried along by the fascination of the clinician for the phenomena he observes. If this judgement seems harsh, then the reader should consult Haley's critique in Framo's (1972) edited book. This was an attempt to establish a dialogue between researchers and therapists, and in his contribution Haley concludes:

'However, if we judge the exploratory work done to date by severe methodological criteria, one can only conclude that the evidence for difference between the normal family and a family containing a patient is no more than indicative.'

Now lest that should seem too gloomy a judgement, we should hasten to add that Haley often goads to further thought by his iconoclasm, perhaps in order to act as a restraint on a remarkable innovative and lively sphere of therapeutic activity.

It is difficult to identify exactly how and when conjoint methods of therapy were first developed, although the intellectual climate was undoubtedly created first by von Bertalanffy's description of general systems theory (to which we, like all others working in this field have already paid obeisance in Chapter 1) and secondly by the remarkable and liberating effect of Lewin's (1948) application of field theory to social problems. This, coupled with the pragmatic urgency to remake the world after the Second World War led to the capacity to liberate therapeutic approaches from the rigid strait-jacket of the 1930s. A fascinating insight into this liberation is given by Dicks (1967) writing as a psychoanalyst experimenting with the 'new' methods. He writes (p. 53):

'It was later in 1949, that I invited my colleague, Dr. Mary Luff to join me in a pilot study. At this stage we still envisaged separate full psychiatric personality assessment by one of us of each spouse as a first approach to a new case, even though we groped towards joint initial appraisal of the couple as the unit of therapy. To this end with some sense of daring[sic !] we instituted the joint interview — a foursome session of both partners with both of us.'

And this in the same year that T. S. Eliot had Sir Henry Harcourt-Reilly doing much more than this on stage in 'The Cocktail Party'!

The therapeutic possibilities for the natural group were too strong (once recognized) to be fettered by the chains of psychotherapeutic tradition although it has required strenuous effort and brave souls to work consistently in this area. One result has been that this field has had an excess, perhaps, of charismatic therapists, forced to be such in order to draw attention to the great advantage of bringing clinical skill into a alliance with the naturally occurring processes rather than the reverse. However, we are now on surer ground.

Within the field of marital therapy it is possible to identify a limited number of practical 'styles' of therapeutic procedure which need some description. Although theoretically their individual strategies are different, in the clinical setting with the couple their differences necessarily become blurred. The therapeutic method forces the therapist to make conceptualizations from the observed behaviour of patient and spouse in order to make any therapeutic gains within the interaction. The most ardent behaviourist is obliged to formulate the process in ways which far exceed the S–R model since he finds the language available to describe individual behavioural units no longer suffices to explain the complexities of the couple's interaction. Behavioural acts in isolation without access to the communicative influence of the internal world of both partners, have little meaning and can become nonsensical.

A simple example may make this clear. A depressed husband was discussing the very real difficulties which he was experiencing in feeling sufficiently worthwhile to believe that his work as a draughtsman was actually possible on a daily basis. In order to deal with this problem the therapist needs a detailed description from both the husband and then the wife about how they handle the challenge or threat of each new working day. Their descriptions would include observations of behaviour and the therapist would soon recognize the covert themes that were governing the specific interchange. The observed pattern of behaviour is then seen as only a part of the process that is being enacted. The therapeutic universe thus consists of both the behavioural acts and their meaning.

## The Patient–Therapist Relationship

This is one part of the therapeutic work which can be specified more closely because it is only capable of a limited number of permutations. It has been the subject of a good deal of controversy, but with very little clear supportive evidence for the efficacy of any particular style of working. The therapist–patient systems which are now recognized are:

1. Conjoint therapy in which the couple are engaged simultaneously in therapeutic work with one or more therapists.
2. The group form of conjoint therapy in which several couples are treated simultaneously by one or more therapists.
3. The collaborative/concurrent therapy in which marital partners are seen separately by different therapists, thus working in different therapeutic settings and not focusing on the shared therapeutic experience of the couple. The therapists collaborate by meeting to discuss their separate therapeutic encounters and may do this alone or in the presence of the couple depending on their

orientation and assessment of the clinical problems. This particular method is the one of choice of the workers at the Institute of Marital Studies in London, and is largely based on their application of object relations theory. (Pincus, 1971).

4. Individual therapy where one spouse seeks help from one therapist and the other from another and totally unrelated therapist.

It will be clear that unless there are theoretical reasons to the contrary (like those which we have just mentioned), the therapy may also be a combination of these methods in order to deal with the emergence of certain problems. Thus it is quite common for conjoint interviews to be interspersed with occasional ordinary dyadic interviews when one partner wants to discuss a particular problem which he/she feels is behaviourally and emotionally neutral for the spouse. This departure would ordinarily be within the contractual arrangement so that discussion of the separate interview would take place at the next conjoint session. Thus the therapist does not get 'trapped by secrets'.

For a more detailed description of the dynamics and management of the conjoint therapy situation the reader is referred to Haley (1963). Here he describes the role definition of the married couple and the rules which become established to govern their behaviour. At another level metarules or rules about rules are set up to provide a second order of control, e.g. although the couple may discuss their problems endlessly their metarule may be never to agree or resolve a problem. Rules may impose an order and a safety within the relationship, but may not serve the interests of each individual equally. Any attempts by one or other partner to change the rules may prove too challenging and the system becomes unable to cope with the stresses it entails. Thus a rigidity of style becomes imposed on their method of relating.

During therapy the aim of the therapist should be to redefine and relabel the observed activity so that opportunities are created for the couple to alter their rules within the safety of the therapeutic setting. Their roles should be interepreted back to them thus giving permission for a redefinition of role relationships to take place. Reassurances can be offered by emphasising the positive sides of the relationship and explaining the partner's behaviour in a positive way, and at the same time accepting their present behaviour uncritically. The therapist learns a great deal about the interaction by tuning in to the non-verbal repertoire and making explicit the covert rules about behaviour which may exist at a non-verbal level. Thus the husband who talks endlessly seems overtly to control the relationship, but at a covert level the quiet submissive wife is controlling most effectively and generating insecurities and tensions in her partner about her participation in the relationship. The therapist needs to give this couple permission to change the rules so that the wife's feelings of dissatisfaction can be made explicit at a verbal level of exchange.

These descriptions and styles of therapy were not designed for work with patients who were primarily depressed and it may appear superficially that the use of such methods implies that the marital conflict or stress is primary, and the experience of depression secondary to it. But this does not fit with our understanding of the emergence of depressive behaviour. The conjoint method (if we may use one term to represent all variants) is based on the assumption that the depressive phenomena will be expressed within the interpersonal context and will therefore be a mutual experience not only of the spouses, but also of the therapist(s). It is important also to say that this does not in any way deny that the acute and extremely unpleasant physical and psychological experiences are part of the core experience of the depressed individual in a way that they can never be for the experience of the spouse or therapist (unless that is, they too develop the same kind of disturbance). That may sound peculiar, but it is not without validity. Coyne's (1976) studies are most interesting in their description of the way in which others respond to the depressed person's communication. The studies are all the more important because they showed that the effect was powerful with complete strangers — a fact that perhaps should not surprise us in the light of the ancient story of Job's comforters!

The therapeutic issues which are most likely to be the focus of attention will involve the central importance of the structure of autonomy and dependence in the marriage. These are most often expressed in terms of role functions (as we have demonstrated in the cases that have been described in this and previous chapters) and the responsibility which the depressed person often feels, but no longer wishes to carry. This frequently implies regressed behaviour on the patient's part of which the most common example is staying in bed. But then if the patient's husband tries to get her up, the wife's ambivalence about her autonomy often comes through in the form of angry complaints about her husband's expectations of her, and even that he is the 'cause' of her needing to retire. But the conflict may then become impossible to resolve because the depressed wife is apparently incapable of sustaining the interaction. Thus the initial covert feelings about dependence are compounded by the couple's overt inability to handle this intensely dependent situation. This (and similar) situations can then be used by the therapist to explore the subtle interrelations between the patient's internal view of herself as a non-functioning woman, and the tendency to project this sense of inadequacy on to both her spouse and her children.

## Problems for the Spouse

Some of the problems for the spouse are well illustrated in Lewinsohn's and Shaeffer's (1975) interesting account of a therapeutic programme in which the patient's spouse and family took part in the family home. Here one of the implicit aims of the therapy was to overcome the initial feeling of helplessness which the family members had developed as a result of trying to cope with the patient's own helpless view of life. This suggests that a potent reason for conjoint approaches to therapy would be to restore to them the sense of hope about their spouse. If we follow our own initial account of the actual emergence of depressive phenomena, it follows that all therapeutic attempts must be based on the intervention by the therapist into the system which has apparently led to the emergence of the depression. With a person who has become gloomy, depressed, depreciating and hopeless over only a very limited time the spouse is inevitably part of this system. Different spouse pairs will have differing levels of tolerance, but once the process of marital recriminations begin, it is likely to be a very short time before the 'long-suffering' spouse defensively withdraws and suffers no more — either from his/her spouses's attacks or from the increasing sense of his/her own guilt and helplessness. There is no available evidence about the length of this period, but it could certainly be as short as a week in some cases.

At this point, the spouse is likely to cut off viable communication in an attempt to safeguard both him/herself and also often their children if they are still young and dependent. This *may* work as a strategy by breaking into the escalating cycle of depressed cognition. But equally — and more likely — it will confirm the cognitive pattern of expectation of rejection already held by the sufferer and intensify the depressive experience. Coyne describes this point as the 'interactive stalemate'. Yet it is in this very situation that all too often, the professional helper (especially a medically trained one) will say that the depression is 'in' the patient, and that his baleful effect on others close to him only 'proves' that this is the case.

Attempted suicide or self injury at this point only reinforces the medical model, but if one takes an interactive view of the act one can see it as an attempt to open up communication at a point of impasse. In fact, in dealing with attempted suicides in association with marital difficulties it is fascinating to see how the dialogue of living can become resumed and how important a time it can be for successful crisis intervention.

### Strategies to Help the Spouse

Thus one of the major aims of conjoint therapy emerges quite clearly, and that is to actually facilitate and enlarge the spouse's sense of being able to be helpful. In a situation where both have become used to a chronic state of angry or hopeless helplessness this may appear a hard task indeed, but it may also be the therapeutic fulcrum for change which both spouses need.

One can intervene by interpreting their needs to each other and clarifying the dynamics of the hostility and resentments which have arisen between them. One thereby changes the rules and disallows the existing roles of non-communication and avoidance. The spouse should be encouraged to express real feelings towards his partner and be aware of the hazards involved in assuming a controlled, tense emotion-free posture. Once the partner interprets that he/she is being treated as though in the sick role this confirms existing anxieties about the relationship.

### An Example of Therapy with a Depressed Couple

The best way to illustrate therapeutic intervention is to give a brief description of how therapy was carried out in a characteristic case. In this couple, the treatment period lasted over about six months and comprised a total of some fifteen sessions. Mr. and Mrs. A were referred together by their family practitioner after Mrs. A had become increasingly depressed over the previous six months. The crisis had occurred one Sunday when Mrs. A had become 'hysterical' and quite uncontrollable. She calmed down rapidly with help from her general practitioner and attended out-patient clinic a few days later.

They described how things had deteriorated since Mrs. A's hysterectomy a year previously. There had been a long post-operative recovery period and she had become increasingly tense and irritable. At the same time she had increased her demands for attention from her husband who (on his own account) was at his wits' end. Mrs. A was greatly relieved to be referred to the clinic since she felt that at last someone was taking her problems seriously. She visualized herself as worthless, felt that she had lost her position in a busy family and was being cast aside by her mother, her husband and indeed everyone who mattered to her. Thus she felt very weepy and low each morning after a poor night's sleep and was soon into a demanding routine with her husband.

At the first interview, Mr. A was anxious to present his wife as the patient, insisting that he had given all he could to make her life more comfortable. This was true; as a self-made businessman he had worked hard with his wife to provide a comfortable home and to enable their children to take opportunities in higher education which neither of them had had. He found his wife's new sexual demands particularly distressing after a previous good adjustment in this area. Now he had become unable to respond to her — which simply increased her feelings of inadequacy and worthlessness. Indeed he felt himself quite disabled by her depressive demand and had become very irritable and tense. He presented himself to the therapist as compliant and almost obsequious, but this manner only partially obscured a fairly evident hostility to the therapist and wife alike. No doubt he experienced a sense of failure at not being able to provide support for his wife over these problems as he had done effectively in the past.

The conjoint therapy task in this case seemed fairly clear. Mrs. A's roles as wife and mother had been based on the premise that she and her husband were sufficient for each other and needed little or no outside help (especially from her own family towards whom she felt particularly bitter). Her hysterectomy symbolized the fact that, for her, this stable system had broken down and neither the role of wife or of mother offered her protection from her long-hidden feelings of personal inadequacy. Now, she patently *was* less than adequate. Her attempts to communicate this to her husband were totally unsuccessful and he felt frustrated and inadequate in his attempts to help her and finally withdrew. Her role as wife was under increasing threat and this simply confirmed her inadequate view of herself.

The first step was to offer the couple a simplified analysis of these dynamics with the emphasis upon the rigidity of their role structure. There were many strengths in their previous relationship and these were used to demonstrate that they had the capacity to develop new ways of communicating with each other with the therapist acting as warm supporter and facilitator if they were willing to try. Mrs. A accepted the formulation and also the contract to try conjoint sessions together, but had reservations about the possible success of these sessions in ameliorating her acute and uncomfortable symptoms. She was relieved at the suggestion that she should continue taking antidepressant medication for immediate symptom relief under the care of her general practitioner. Mr. A was much more dubious about the formulation and therapy proposals, but was persuaded that even if he could not accept or understand his own part in the system, that he would nevertheless learn a great deal in the joint sessions which would help him with his own feeling of utter helplessness in the face of his wife's depression. This he could accept, and agreed to a limited series of six sessions at weekly intervals with review after a month.

From then on the same therapist took primary responsibility for treatment including occasional consultations between the family doctor and the therapist and the family doctor and the couple. During the first sessions the key issues were Mrs. A's anger at her husband's inability to accept that he was ever wrong or made mistakes, together with her own belief that she was the victim in her own family of origin. At first Mr. A dealt with his wife's anger by telling her that this was 'really' due to her depression for which he had a quite different explanation. But she insisted, bringing into the therapy session incidents not from their past life, but from their present experience. This resulted in him becoming both emotionally distressed and also more experientially involved in the therapeutic experience. In fact, his 'rightness' was much more a pathetic need on his part to be able to explain everything in a clear and rational manner (to himself) rather than the overweening sense of his own superiority which his wife imagined. Thus his wife's view of his adequacy was in many ways just the reverse, and therefore her angry feelings were considerably misplaced. This, too, became part of the therapeutic work. In Chapter 5 we referred to one of our research findings which was that when the spouse of the depressed patient is the husband, he may well have considerable difficulties in adapting his role behaviour to his apparently intensely dependent wife and that this may make her recovery more difficult. This was exactly so in the case of the As in that Mr. A had great difficulty in meeting his wife's dependency needs initially. He had accepted her as a symmetrical partner (albeit a little 'weak'), but not the fact that she now depended on him for her very existence.

Conjoint therapy, then, continued for the scheduled time, but with considerable oscillations. Mrs. A's initially strong feelings about her victimization by her own family receded rapidly as she expressed more of her marital problems. The hysterectomy too became quite unimportant except as a landmark dating the beginning of the difficulties. During the difficult periods Mr. A now accepted gratefully the therapist's presence as an experienced helper who enabled him to feel much less helpless when his wife was depressed, and therefore paradoxically more able to allow her to be dependent upon him. At the end of the scheduled six sessions there was considerable improvement both symptomatically and interpersonally. However they both requested more sessions on the basis that they still felt relatively insecure with each other. A new six-week contract was therefore arranged which included opportunities for Mrs. A to explore her own perceived social inadequacy (which she no longer blamed either on her depression or her husband) in the face of the re-alignments which her life was requiring. The sessions were therefore alternated between conjoint therapy with the couple and individual sessions with Mrs. A. This proved effective and she worked well at recognizing her own difficulties and rehearsing steps which she could actually take to shift her role into an altogether more satisfying one. The therapy was terminated by the couple going away on a fairly lavish and highly successful holiday. By this time her drug intake had just about ceased, and although they both reported problems at follow-up interviews, they felt that they were now back with a more symmetrical relationship, but this time with considerable flexibility.

### Conjoint Therapy and Depression

We need to make it clear at this point that this case proves nothing about the efficacy of this treatment mode compared with others. In Chapter 5 we have already discussed the potential influence of antidepressant medication. Mrs. A had shown little response to this form of treatment over the preceding six months but we did not attempt to displace drug treatment with another treatment mode. The antidepressant may well have influenced Mrs. A's personal emotional experience, but at a time when she was unable to use this change because of the complex psychological issues involved. Further, that defining the problem as simply one person's 'depression' was preventing the couple from either accepting another formulation or attempting to work out solutions.

The details of the A's life together illustrates the importance of a life event in precipitating difficulties in a relationship which lacks the resources to provide a close intimate relationship at times of stress. These factors led to the clinical state described so clearly as 'diffuse misery' and illustrated the rapid establishment of impaired communication and the emergence of overt (rather than covert) hostile friction between the spouse and the wider family.

The main therapeutic problem for the therapist at the outset is to present the procedure to the couple as a reasonable one. We have ourselves discussed the complex set of ideas which lie behind our formulation, but this has to be redefined to the patient and spouse in a comprehensible and common sense way which they can accept. To quote Coleridge's felicitous phrase, it may be necessary to ask them to exercise 'that willing suspension of disbelief for the moment, which constitutes poetic[therapeutic] faith'. This was certainly the case with Mr. A, but it fortunately happened that the pathology of their interaction was so easy to demonstrate to them that 'initial disbelief' soon became experienced fact. This is certainly easier to demonstrate to the couple than some other, more esoteric explanations of human behaviour! It will also not have escaped the reader that as the therapy proceeded with the As some sessions of dyadic therapy with one spouse alone were interspersed with the conjoint sessions. But the important thing to note here is that these sessions were mutually agreed by the therapeutic trio as being the proper way to facilitate the joint therapeutic process. This is quite different from agreeing to see one spouse for therapy before the other spouse has accepted a therapeutic role.

What we have tried to do in discussing the case of Mr. and Mrs. A is to exemplify the way in which this particular form of working matched some of the more general findings in which an interpersonal view of depression was offered as the important framework for basic understanding of depression.

So far we have put forward the case that the disturbances associated with depressive phenomena are very frequently marital and family related. This is partly because clinical depression seems to occur very frequently in married patients. It is difficult in these days of subtle and complex understanding of the interweaving of many aetiological factors in psychological disturbance to argue forcefully one way or the other. But we can say that the most recon research, including our own, points to marital experiences as crucial variables in the onset, development and probably treatment of depressive disorder. At the very least, the depressed person's spouse is significantly affected by the problem, at the most he or she may be completely interwoven in the problem at a behavioural, interpersonal and symbolic level. This view is in marked contrast to that held only a few years ago, which resulted in the therapeutic offerings being based exclusively on either a monadic psychological or pharmacological/physical model.

By definition the conjoint method is a psychological rather than a biological one, but it does enable the therapist to deal with a fairly wide range of phenomena, and makes it possible for the therapeutic work to be easily extended from the clinic into the home without the actual physical presence of the therapist. We may learn a good deal from experiments like Lewinsohn's in which the therapist spent a lot of time in the home but in clinical practice it would not be feasible for the most part. Despite this, the therapist in conjoint therapy can explore three dimensions of the problem; the separate experience of each spouse and the actual joint experience occurring in the therapy setting. Thus, for instance, with the therapist's help, the 'normal' spouse can articulate the powerful emotional effect which the depressed spouse is producing. Usually this partner is unable to express these feelings for fear of the consequences and the possible harm that may be caused to the 'sick' partner. There are powerful and frightening messages in the downcast dejected and fearful posture of the depressed individual which have both a warning and demanding quality at the same time.

But having made a reasonable strong clinical and research case for the application of conjoint techniques, we need to ask what other evidence there is about their efficacy. The most important study to date is one by Friedman (1975). It is important because at the present time it is the only study known to us which specifically tests the application of the conjoint method to depressed couples. Friedman compared drug therapy and marital therapy alone and in combination. But even in such a simple comparison the potential differences are quite remarkably complex, and like all other studies which are more than correlational, the factors involved are intricate. The 196 patients were offered both a drug or placebo and either minimal contact therapy (half an hour at two-weekly intervals approximately) or marital therapy (one hour weekly). Unfortunately the two forms of psychotherapy were not equated for time spent with the therapist.

The results of a global assessment scale are shown in Table 6.1. This was a 6-point scale in the study which has been collapsed to three here because the 'worse' categories contain very few subjects. For the whole study population the overall global improvement rates are 75% improved, 19% no change, and 6% worse. Thus, the whole study was a very successful one in terms of global improvement over twelve weeks.

From our point of view it would have been very interesting to have known what the differential rates were for men and women, but since only 20% of the patients were men the author felt that this was not a large enough proportion to make any firm statements. But the author is quite firm in his overall assessment of the results, and he writes 'it is quite clear then that the conjoint marital psychotherapy condition in this study had a positive effect on symptom relief and clinical improvement, and

**Table 6.1**

*Global improvement score for depressed patients (from Friedman, 1975, collapsed data) %*
*(over 12 weeks)*

|  | Improved | No Change | Worse | Total |
|---|---|---|---|---|
| Drug/Marital Therapy | 89 | 11 | 0 | 100 |
| Drug/Minimum Therapy | 68 | 23 | 9 | 100 |
| Placebo/Marital Therapy | 75 | 19 | 6 | 100 |
| Placebo/Minimum Therapy | 67 | 22 | 11 | 100 |

$N. = 196$

that some of this effect occurred as early as four weeks ...'.

The detailed scales in the paper give the very subtle ways in which the treatments were more or less effective both between the beginning and the end of the treatment programme as well as at some intermediate times. Unfortunately Friedman only reports on the defined time limits of the study and no follow-up data is available. Though this does not invalidate the importance of these findings, it does not offer the opportunity for long term comparisons.

One particularly important aspect of Friedman's findings is that the marital therapy may initially worsen some aspects of the patient's relationship with the spouse as the therapist focuses on some of the conflict areas of their joint lives. He suggests that this is where drug treatment may be particularly useful in combination with psychotherapy in taking the edge off some of the very unpleasant personal symptoms of depression in a situation in which, initially things do not appear to be improving at all. In the drug and minimal therapy condition the reverse actually seemed to happen. That is to say that after quite a short period the patient was moving to a significantly more positive view of his/her spouse, but that this effect was considerably diminished by the end of the longer period.

Friedman comments on this point in discussing the implications which the study has for treatment planning. He says (p. 635):

'These differential treatment effects pose the following question regarding the patient's future: is the fact that the depressed patients learned to assert themselves against their mates and to express their negative feelings directly going to be good or bad for them, in the long term, compared to patients treated with drugs? ... Our own speculation on this issue is that the marital therapy patients may have gained some assurance against future relapses into depression in the future ... According to this formulation a key question for the spouse would be whether he or she would prefer the burden of having a partner who gets "sick" from time to time to having a partner who would assert herself or himself more and possible disagree more often in the marital relationship ...'

Finally it is most interesting to note that the results from this study compare very favourably indeed with two recent studies of psychotherapy with depressed patients. In both of these (Klerman and DiMascio, 1973; Covi and coworkers, 1973) the approach was dyadic or group therapy and the contribution of psychotherapy appeared to be only slight. In view of the fact that Friedman's patients were not selected for the presence of especially pathological marriages, the results are even more striking. From the point of view of this chapter, the study would have touched excellence if it had included some analysis of the well spouse's own experience and perception of his depressed partner. However that perhaps would be asking too much in an already highly sophisticated and complex piece of research.

## Differential Therapy with Depressed Husbands and Wives

As we near the end of this discussion, one matter on which we have so far said little is the way that conjoint therapy will differ according to the sex of the patient. At the beginning we commented on the paucity of studies on the individual and social psychology of depressed men. In general, all depressed patients have been lumped together regardless of sex. This seems to have been another instance of the ever-compelling pressure to reify the phenomena that patients describe, and so assume that one man's suicidal thoughts are really identical to another woman's wishes for her own demise. And so long as explanation remains in the intrapsychic realms perhaps that is justified — although even the clinical experience of listening to people of the two sexes express similar ideas of worthlessness, guilt, and helplessness is remarkably different. Indeed, the sex of the clinician will obviously also have a significant effect on the encounter. Most people (clinicians included) find it more difficult to accept the often pathetic distress of the depressed man than the similar distress in the depressed woman. Role prescriptions for behaviour are very powerful in their effect even on a practitioner who has a good deal of knowledge about his own implicit responses and judgements.

This suggests that it may be extremely valuable (if something of a therapeutic luxury) to have two therapists of opposite sex working with a couple. Certainly the need for this has been highlighted in recent years with the sharpening of therapeutic methods to deal with sexual problems. But often, there is no choice, and therefore the issue of the sex of the patient becomes more important than the sex of the therapist. It may simply be, for example, that if the therapist is a woman she is more likely to have some experience of depression herself and thus initially perhaps is more sympathetic to the patient (or less sympathetic if the reverse is the case).

Thus the question of gender already appears an important one for both patient and clinician. But if we put aside the problems associated with the therapist, then how should we expect that conjoint therapy would differ depending upon the gender of the depressed person? First of all it is more difficult to involve the non-patient husbands of patient wives in therapy for a number of simple practical reasons. Work commitments may be seen as increasingly important at a time when his partner is incapacitated. He may be struggling to double-up as father and mother at home or may need to find a substitute for his wife's previous role. His wife's therapist may collude with him by agreeing that his depressed wife is a great 'burden' and that his role now is to keep the ship afloat until his wife recovers. Thus in the therapeutic work he may actually be quite passive. Our own research also tends to suggest that depressed wives remain more ambivalent towards their husbands and have much more difficulty in once again taking up their caring and nurturing role. But also if the husband becomes too effective in the household roles, his wife can feel displaced and this can act antitherapeutically by highlighting her own devalued view of herself.

So the situation all-too-readily becomes one in which the husband's stake in the therapy becomes that of coping until recovery comes — as of course it nearly always does. Yet Friedman's study also shows that it is possible to involve husbands in a treatment programme with a little effort. He and his colleagues only lost a negligible number of subjects through the spouse's unwillingness to cooperate. Obviously this capacity to enter into some kind of therapeutic relationship will crucially depend on the premorbid quality of the marriage and the significance of the depressive episode to that relationship. Recent evidence suggests (without again unfortunately any discrimination by gender) that where there is a negative response on the part of the spouse, then relapse among hospitalized married patients is significantly more likely to occur (Vaughn and Leff, 1976). This of course suggests that therapeutic work with the spouse is even *more* important with those who are reluctant than with those who are more willing.

It may well be that the woman was working prior to her disturbance, and there is some evidence from Weissman and Paykel's (1974) study that this has a positive effect on recovery. As much as anything this must be due to the fact that the family will have already organized its daily affairs in order to cope with the joint work of both spouses and that her diminished capacity is less obvious both to herself and to the family. In addition to this, the wife's working life is less likely than that of her husband to be the one in which the perceived loss or threat of loss (which is a very common part of the aetiology of the disturbance) has occurred. Thus, although she may initially feel just as helpless a worker as she does a mother or wife, the lack of conflict in that situation may create it's own therapeutic conditions, and enable her to return quite rapidly to not only performing competently but also feeling that she does so. This in turn often has a generalizing effect and enables the woman to experience an increasing sense of worth and self-esteem at home.

## Differences between Husbands and Wives

On the basis of role structure alone and without regard to any other aspect of masculinity it would be very likely that depressed husbands would differ in their mode of becoming depressed. Emphasis on intrapsychic phenomena and core symptoms of depression have been with us for so long that it has blinded us to the social and existential differences which occur between depressed men and depressed women. At the present time there is a dearth of research material upon which we can base a firm understanding of conjoint work with husbands, but some understanding — albeit of a limited kind — arises out of clinical experience which is still valuable in formulating an approach.

In an interesting discussion of the psychodynamics of the more severe forms of depression, Arieti (1974) uses the concept of the 'dominant other' to explain how the depressed person tends to organize his/her life experiences. He suggests that this dominant other is often a particular person, but may also be an organization or institution of some kind, which has become anthropomorphized for this purpose. This is of great importance for men because of their much more powerful emotional investment in their work as a source of gratification than is generally the case for women. Indeed, we have even suggested that for some women competence at work may be an important part of the recovery process, and facilitate increasing competence in other areas of life. The presence, therefore, of a dominant other which is an institution will be an important part of the therapeutic approach to many depressed men and yet still be amenable to change within the marital system.

Obviously the withdrawing and disabling process will be different for men if they become acutely depressed, but the focus of this process is still highly likely to be their home. Perhaps the important difference which is immediately obvious is that it is the setting *to* which, rather than *from* which they will withdraw. This is not necessarily the case, but it is the characteristic which is most likely to distinguish the results of their depressed behaviour from that of women. The same phenomena are also to be observed when a man becomes unemployed and has to base the whole of his life on his home rather than just his domestic and leisure hours. In this situation a transient depressive episode is quite common and the situational dynamics are obviously rather similar. But the depressed man has more to contend with than simply involuntary loss of work and these are the factors which a therapist will be attending to.

One of these factors is that of his masculinity to which we have referred above. Modern men are required to develop this aspect of themselves largely in the areas of work and of sexual relationships, and make self-esteem is often built around these two areas of experience. Home may also be a source of masculine self-esteem, but also in relation to his work in that setting as well — even though it is his own creative work that he does there. Thus acts towards his wife (at both the caring and the love-making levels) and within his work will be important confirmation of his masculinity. This maleness may also contain important elements of emotional control which allow him to express himself fully only in the most intimate parts of his life. The development of depressive pathology may well negate all these sources of a well-being one by one. Often, sexual responses are the first things to diminish, followed by an intensified and increasingly labile form of emotional self-expression or an intense emotional apathy. Concomitantly, work performance falls off and now the depressed man is ready for complete withdrawal.

The therapist now is faced with the task of helping the patient to locate the 'dominant other' but then to bring this into focus in conjoint therapy. It is unlikely that the sufferer's wife will refuse to participate unless the conflict between them is already intense, and it is also unlikely that the covert issues will be the ambivalent ones of autonomy and dependence as is so often the case with women. This permits many wives to adopt a nurturing role — at least in the early stages — which makes them the therapeutic allies of the therapist. It does seem to be the case that men express more feelings of personal worthlessness than women, which avoids the destructive spiral of blame and guilt into which wives often enter. But this may also mean that the males have difficulty in accepting conjoint therapy since they see themselves as responsible for the situation. However this is a depressive concept which actually intensifies their problems rather than solves it, and one which conjoint therapy can effectively challenge.

From then on the two processes of therapy often proceed along similar lines. We have discussed the way in which the focus of depressive cognition will vary both individually in the sense that each person's experience will give them different foci for their action and also along sex roles because of the crucial part played by gender. But the therapeutic process will be the same delicate balance between the inner experience of the patient and the sharing of that experience by both therapist and spouse together. Indeed, it is often the case that critics of this approach argue that depression *is* such a private world of distress that it is wrong to make the suffering person share these experiences with someone as close to him as his spouse. Our argument would be that it is precisely *because* they appear to be so private that they need to be shared.

## Conclusion

In this chapter we have argued the case for a very different approach to psychological therapy with depressed couples. There is consistent evidence that the marital situation is crucial to the understanding of a depressed spouse and that those phenomena which we so often label as belonging to one person are only understandable within the marital context. This is in line with general trends amongst therapeutic approaches, which make more and more use of the naturally occurring relationships which patients already have when they consult us for help. But we hope that we have not been doctrinaire in our statements about how much conjoint therapy should be done. Only each therapist's skill and professional situation can really determine that, and there is plenty of healthy experimentation at the present time. Obviously more research evaluation of such methods is needed, but this is a notoriously difficult and lengthy process which should not prevent therapists from using conjoint methods of their choice. For too long we have been debating the rival claims of intrapsychic theories when the essential interpersonal nature of depression has been staring us in the face. Perhaps the material we have presented here will now give a fillip to further advance in what has already become a major psychotherapeutic task in modern urban society and open up a much broader understanding of the role of depression as perhaps the marital pathology par excellence.

# 7

# THE EFFECTS OF THE DEPRESSED
# PATIENT ON THE FAMILY

So far we have focused exclusively on the dyadic system represented by the marital pair but in this chapter we will enlarge the system to include other family members and consider their response to major disturbance and disequilibrium within the family group.

When one deals with the depressed patient it is very easy to lose sight of the repercussions that are occurring in relation to the other individuals in their immediate environment or home. So often individuals are seen away from the home situation within the consulting room or office and a few superficial enquires about health of the children can be enough to satisfy the conscience of the therapist. It is a relief to learn that granny or a neighbour is helping out and has taken responsibility for the daily life of the family group and one does not need to look more intimately at the bond between parents and child and enquire about its quality or effectiveness, either as a means of communication or to provide for the emotional needs of the children concerned. We cannot ignore the inevitable impact that disturbance between husband and wife represents in terms of the feelings and behaviour generated within the rest of the family.

Let us first consider what we understand by depressed behaviour and put it within the framework of communication. Thus we are not concerned for the internal feeling state of the individual or the intrapsychic conflicts which may be at the root of their disturbance, but are describing the effect their behaviour has on others in terms of how they are seen, experienced and interpreted. How does one feel the depressive quality of another person's behaviour? We are concerned for the here and now, the moment by moment awareness and appraisal, of another's repertoire of behavioural cues. This conceptualization helps us to pinpoint the immediate importance of the communicative aspects of depressive behaviour. The depressive's external appearance may well set the scene giving a message of drabness, lack of interest or concern either for themselves or others. This is conveyed by a lack of postural tone, little responsiveness of facial expression, a reduction in the use of eye-contact and a diminution in expressive movements and gestures generally. In addition there may be the physical apathy of psychomotor retardation or the restlessness and distractibility of the agitated depressive who plucks, rubs or scratches himself in a self pre-occupied and 'autistic' fashion. The non-verbal message therefore is one of self pre-occupation and remoteness; a 'leave me alone' feeling or 'I can't cope with what you are saying' feeling. At other times there can be a great need for a dependency expressed and the depressive appears childlike and clinging, looking for reassurances at both verbal and non-verbal levels.

At a verbal level the depressive communicates self pre-occupation and a concern for negatively toned topics, employing either slow speech broken by long pauses or a stream of agitated phrases. There is a tension in their vocal characteristics and their use of language, which is accompanied by little use of tension relievers such as laughter or humour in their speech.

The interactant immediately becomes cautious and wary, censoring his own words and actions and matching his mood to the individual before him. There is a sense of 'this person is different, damaged or sick in some way and must be treated with care and consideration'. When this is realized an artificiality comes into the relationship and the depressive receives the message back that he or she is expected to be different and cannot be related to in the old ways. Tensions arise between them despite attempted reassurances and expressions of affection and a stalemate arises where neither partner feels they are able to make a real communication with the other, and the depressed individual continues to be pre-occupied with morbid thoughts and a heightened sense of self-blame for the world that they seem to have built around themselves.

Feelings of ambivalence towards their partners arise on both sides, and lead to a pattern of care, concern, rejection and hostility, followed by a sense of despair and guilt which increases the tensions and prejudices the next overtures and continues the upward course of the spiral.

Coyne (1976) demonstrated the effects that a depressed individual could have on a stranger after a series of experimental telephone conversations with each other. The depressed patient induced negative effect and feelings of rejection in the controls with whom they interacted. This quality made them aggressive and unattractive and reduced the effects of their adaptive attempts to appear sociable and acceptable.

However, in this chapter we are looking at a wider social system than the two person couple and are using the understandings we have gained from a consideration of the couple and applying them to specific relationships within the intimate family group or network.

Ackerman (1958) describes the 'biosocial organisation of behaviour' and sees the family as a 'flexible unit that adapts delicately to influences acting upon it from without and within'. The changes within the family relate to the biological bonds of men and women, mother and child, and these bonds can be strengthened or weakened at critical times in the family life. He sees shifts within the family as generating tensions, frustrations and feelings of hostility and resentment. The interchange of feelings between members revolves around this oscillation between love and hate.

Using the language of systems theory we can say that the family system has flexibilities within it which make it capable of absorbing and dealing with a certain level of stresses and strains. The family equilibrium becomes reset at a different level of functioning and a new homeostasis or stability becomes established. When depressive symptoms emerge in one family member we see this is an indication that the system has been unable to re-establish itself completely and that there may be interactive regidities present which have made a new symptom-free stability an impossibility. The depressed family member then 'carries' the symptom on behalf of the rest of the family group and this is an indication that the system is still vulnerable though has made a new equilibrium for itself. Ackerman emphasizes the biological survival value that is built into a natural system such as a family so that there is a drive or instinctive need to protect itself from internal or external threats.

The changed family equilibrium can have subtle though profound effects on intimate interpersonal relationships so that there may be little awareness of the change that is being effected. It is always easier to focus on the obvious, which is the depressed parent who channels attention, care and feelings of hostility and rejection on to themselves. How do individual families rationalize their dilemmas and deal with the depressed member?

The depressed person must be relegated to a new role so that he or she can continue to contribute some part of their important biological function as a parent whether it be for nurturing, developmental reasons, as an identity figure for the next generation, or to continue to take their role as a spouse. However, at the same time the family must also shift their roles to complement and give credibility to the depressive's new position.

A Marriage Guidance Counsellor writing anonymously about her own and her families' experience of a depressed husband and father after twenty years of stable and well adjusted living, uses the following description of it:

> 'The family, although very concerned and helpful, also found it difficult to understand and rather frightening to see him reduced to such a state'.
>
> 'The three eldest returned to University with a mixture of reluctance and relief and they wanted me to keep them fully informed'.
>
> 'In the beginning we felt guilty when we were cheerful and Bill was depressed; we did not know how to react for the best — whether to comfort, encourage, ignore, jolly him out of it (impossible!) or what. The family have admitted to feeling angry that Dad was such a wet blanket at times, but also to hating themselves for feeling it. It is difficult for children to see their father cry or behave in a strange way and their reactions will depend on their age and stage of development.'
>
> 'One can feel desperately alone when one's partner has to be protected from worry and it is easy to feel childishly in need of support and comforting when all the help and attention seems to be focused on the ill partner and the family forgotten.'

In this account she communicates clearly her own and her family's negative feelings towards her husband, together with their feelings of shame and guilt and frustrations at not knowing how to help him. She dealt with the problem by devoting herself to his care and helping him stage by stage through the tortuous paths of a three-year depressive experience and tried where possible to shield her family from her own anxieties. This is one way of dealing with the problem, but in other families the problem is contained or extruded by different behavioural devices. The family makes adaptations in its pattern and style of living to absorb new stresses and changing influences that are impinging on it.

There may be a closing of the ranks with an attempt to cover over and hide the points of vulnerability and difficulty in intrafamilial relationships. A rigid style of acceptable behaviour is imposed upon the family group which protects it from self discovery and self confrontation. The sense of family loyalty is preserved by a papering over of the cracks which produces the desired end result of a show of social respectability and moral strength which allows the family unit to function within its wider social network with the correct stamp of approval and acceptance. Within family members a conspiracy of non-expressiveness and nonquestioning grows up so that certain areas of their emotional life are never expressed, discussed or understood.

It is within this sort of family that the depressed parent can be shielded and protected. His/her depressed behaviour exhibits itself at intervals, but is quickly dealt with and concealed once again by a further patching up and rallying round. The behaviour may manifest itself by a build-up of tensions and irritations and there may be further timid and futile attempts at self-expression which become inhibited by a sense of guilt, shame and badness about their actions. At times tensions may reach a fever pitch and produce isolated outbursts of hostility and on occasions frankly aggressive behaviour, especially where the male parent is involved. So often there is a concern and caring shown at a verbal level in these families, but their non-verbal communications are in direct conflict. Relationships tend to be fear governed, approval must be gained for family acceptance and rejection is the fate of the intrepid member who dares to become the scapegoat and step outside the family's rules. These dynamics are not operating at a conscious level yet subtly control and influence family loyalties and ties. Self-expression becomes a family problem and there is encouragement for denial of feelings and a feeling of unacceptability for the depressed style of behaviour. The best way of illustrating all this is to take a case history, and the H. family serves to illustrate much of this pattern.

The H's presented to the psychiatric services as a result of their third child and youngest daughter taking an overdose at the age of 23. She described clearly that although she had lived away from her family for years, she was still intensely involved and preoccupied with the family problems at home and as a result had not been able to develop her own independent sense of identity. She described her father who was now in his fifties, who had been depression prone for years, and who had outbursts of irritable and aggressive behaviour and at one time had been physically punitive towards her in childhood. She had an overwhelming need to seek his approval and affection and saw him as a potentially warm individual who always rejected her approaches and cast her back repeatedly leaving her with the feeling that she must be bad and unlovable.

Her mother, in contrast, was a very capable controlling figure who dominated the household and overshadowed her daughter's development by her own accomplishments. Mrs. H was aware of rationing her affections between her three children and recalled a conscious decision to restrict her open display of feeling for her younger daughter at the time when she was a plump rosy cheeked 3 year old, in order to give time to her less demanding and more shut-off 7 year old daughter.

In general they were a physically and sexually inhibited family. Mr. H, despite being openly provocative, resentful and critical of his wife, nevertheless had developed a considerable dependence upon her strength and energies. However, he showed a greater sensitivity than his wife and was at all times very aware of the needs of his children and able to give a perceptive account of their individual difficulties, but at no time was he able to intervene and be guided by his own feelings. In the work situation he lacked confidence and had allowed opportunities for promotion to pass him by, preferring the security of a simpler, less demanding job. There was also evidence of considerable pathology in the lives of their two older children. At the time of their daughter's breakdown they were concerned, but once again unable to meet her emotional demand and resorted to skating over the areas of difficulty.

But there are other family patterns unlike the Hs in which the behaviour of the depressed parent is very much a central issue and focus for the family's adaptations and activities. In these families the parent is labelled sick and extruded as an important figure from the family's organization. Repeated hospitalizations may contribute to this picture and lend their confirmation to the establishment of the sick role. The 'well' partner has to take over primary responsibility for the daily life of the family and finds strength in the resulting martyred role which they establish for themselves. This brings them a new sense of authority and importance in relation to the wider social network and can lead to difficulties in once more admitting the 'sick' member to an active part in the family system. The 'well' parent is also the key figure in relation to the children and may form a possessive or peer relationship with them. As a result new alliances are set up and patterns of loyalty changed and adaptations made to changed and more powerful role positions. To illustrate this pattern we will turn to another case history which is that of Mr. and Mrs. B.

Mrs. B is a woman in her middle thirties who has had repeated depressive episodes associated with high levels of anxiety over a 7 year period since a hysterectomy in her late twenties. She had experienced an emotionally insecure, though sexually satisfactory, relationship with her husband before this time. The threat of sexual unattractiveness as a result of her operation precipitated her into a dependent and regressed marital relationship during which time she took repeated small overdoses and made hysterical demands for attention and support. She became phobic and experienced difficulties in dealing with her domestic role. Her two daughters grew through their late childhood and early adolescent years experiencing an inadequate, petulant and critical mother and despite their anxieties for her, soon learnt that their strong, lively intelligent and active father provided a more consistent and secure identity figure for them. He could also be youthful, flirtatious and indulgent with them. They established peer relationships with him and flouted their mother's feeble attempts at authority and the long time that the patient took to stabilize and re-assert herself at home related to her feelings of extrusion and rejection by her husband and daughters.

In addition to these two patterns there is a third type of family in which the depressed parent denies her/his feelings of depression and responds to the experiences of frustration and alienation from other family members by hostile defensive and sometimes paranoid manoeuvres. Their defences become a powerful weapon with which they can intimidate and reject the approaches of family members and justify their position by accusations of disloyalty and mistrust. They become increasingly bitter as they become more isolated both emotionally and sexually and blame the family for becoming remote from them. The C. family will serve to illustrate this final pattern.

Mr. C, a man in his middle thirties, had always been a hypersensitive and impetuous man, prone to reject relationships when difficulties presented. He had the capacity to hold stubbornly and exclusively to a point of view and feared appearing the loser in his relationships with women. He had become increasingly depressed and self pre-occupied and had experienced great concern at a loss of sexual feeling. At the same time he blamed his wife for his predicament, seeing her as a smug housewife who did not support him in his business endeavours, and also rejected him for his poor sexual performance and monopolised their children. He greeted her pleas for understanding by an angry silence, demanding time to himself and refusing to become involved in domestic affairs. He became very critical of his 8 year old son, noting his lack of physical prowess and blaming his wife's family for their genetic influence. This boy was becoming tense and anxious in his bid to please his father. As the isolation and feelings of depression increased he became suspicious of Mrs. C's behaviour, accusing her of an extramarital entanglement which justified his feelings of mistrust. The two younger children saw little of their father and became frightened by his angry critical outbursts when they did meet him. Gradually he was able to admit his need for his wife's concern and to let go of his angry, hostile position, acknowledging his self-induced isolation and the resulting feelings of depression.

## Effects on Children

In each of the three family types that we have described there has been a pattern of disturbed marital relationships but difficulties have also been expressed through the children's behaviour. Children can be used by their parents as figures to be possessed or rejected as objects for transference of ambivalent feelings generated by other key figures. Other writers have been very involved with this point of view and include Winnicott (1971) who writes that 'the child's symptomatology reflects illness in one or both of the parents or in the social situation and it is this which needs attention. It may be the child who best puts us in touch with the principal defect in the environment'. He sees the depressed mother's initial difficulties as arising from ambivalence and guilt in relation to her child. In more extreme situations Resnich 1969) in reviewing filicide found that 71 % of the mothers were depressed and the victim was frequently the 'favoured child of a loathed spouse'.

Another way of understanding this problem is to describe the child as the scapegoat' of the family. Boszormenyi-Nagy and Sparks (1973) use this model in order to elaborate their dialectic ideas of invisible family loyalties. The scapegoat is exploited by other family members and can serve a function as the martyred individual who alleviates the sense of guilt of others and thereby preserves a 'negative loyalty' and togetherness of the family group. Family models and ideas like this can be so rigid and inflexible that they become very difficult to change, but as Skynner (1975) says at least if they are recognizable they are capable of change. More difficult are the 'innumerable habits of evasion, avoidance and subtle distortion of the truth that the child incorporates as part of his own inner model'.

But what are the important variables which have a contrary effect on the developing child? Does the length of the depression in time make a great difference or can harm be produced in a short period of disturbance? Which are the parental characteristics in depression which disturb the family dynamics? From our experience we view repeated depressive episodes or chronicity of depressive behaviour as a major factor. The small child can accept the emotional or physical withdrawal of its mother for a limited time providing she supplies an adequate substitute during her absence and returns able to reassure her child with a lively responsive caring repertoire of behaviour. However, if she is taken repeatedly into hospital or has a series of depressive episodes which make her emotionally remote and inaccessible for long periods of time, the child becomes sensitized to a repeated sense of loss and rejection which generates separation anxiety so that the child makes an angry or phobic dependency demand on its mother and reacts vigorously to later separations. He/she seeks continually for maternal approval and may set up a cycle of relationship testing whereby dependency demands are increased to the point where rejection becomes inevitable and the mother becomes overwhelmed by her own personal sense of guilt and failure. The child's anxieties may be revealed in other relationships and fields of endeavour, from nightmares and clinging behaviour, to tantrums, school refusal and later delinquency and sexual promiscuity.

Rutter (1972) pointed this out in his review of the literature on maternal deprivation. He too highlights the importance of the quality of the mother's responsiveness in dealing with her child and sees quantity of time spent together as less important. He feels that the mother–child bond can be kept alive at times of separation by appropriate behaviour from mother substitutes and emphasises the importance of continuity of care whether by a parent or surrogate figure. Separation and bond disruption are separate issues and he concludes that separation need not lead to disruption and that more importance should be given to the influence of the rest of the family and the child's own individual contribution to the family interactions. He sees bond disruption, therefore, as the key to suffering and disturbance in the child and supports the idea that its effects are greater where previous bonding has been disturbed by parental conflict or marital turmoil.

A young mother in her early thirties vividly illustrated this when she described her feelings about her three children after she had recovered from a depression which had lasted for two years. She reproached herself for wasting that period of time by not engaging in meaningful activities with them. She had been happy to hand over responsibilities for initiative and leadership to her husband. Her small daughter had virtually become the grandparent's child and her elder son had been anxious and failing at school. She had been insensitive to his needs and had criticized him during that period for being dull and physically unattractive and had blamed herself for his poor physical features. In contrast she had approved of her second son for his superficial good looks and he had subsequently become a spoilt attention-seeking child. After her recovery she was able to take a bright and responsive interest in their progress in the hope that she could compensate for the lost years.

In a searching investigation of psychiatric families, Rutter (1966) demonstrated the effects of inadequate bond formation in his study of the children of sick parents and came to the conclusion that longstanding psychiatric illness was a powerful influence in disturbing the family as a whole, since it was usually associated with chronic marital conflict which had a greater effect than the actual psychiatric symptoms of the patient member. Persistent neurotic illness seemed to have a greater influence, therefore, on family behaviour than recurrent psychotic illnesses. Interaction difficulties between parents can disturb and distort the social and emotional aspects of child care and affect the family's social and recreational life to a major degree. He found that there were great differences in children's individual susceptibilities to mental illness. Boys were more vulnerable than girls and produced higher levels of overt neurotic and antisocial behaviour. In his later study which we have already discussed, Rutter describes the temperament of the vulnerable child as the 'emotionally intense child who is slow to adapt to new situations, is irregular in sleeping, eating and bowel habits and who predominantly produces a negative mood response'. The level of disturbance is also greater where both parents are psychiatrically disturbed and where the same sexed parent is ill because the need for identity and modelling is an important determining factor in the child. He comments also that the parental absence and the disturbed parental presence can both be harmful. Rutter also describes the greater damage produced by longstanding marital discord where affection is lacking rather than the immediate effect of parents separating or divorcing. In the same way chronic physical illness can have a greater disruptive effect on the child's intellectual and emotional development through longstanding family disturbance than can the event of death itself.

The importance of long term disturbed behaviour patterns must be emphasized. In our own study of depressed couples (which we describe in detail in Chapter 5) we were able to show a greater change in the patterns of responsiveness of couples where longstanding interactional difficulties existed, compared with other couples where a good pre-marital relationship seemed to go a long way towards assisting the spouse to deal with the current disturbance more effectively. The same is important in considering parent–child relationships. Mishler and Waxler (1968) in their study of patterns of behaviour in families of young schizophrenics were able to show different styles of responsiveness in schizophrenic families both with their normal and schizophrenic children compared with the responsiveness of a series of normal families and their children. Thus they saw the child's disturbed behaviour using a responsiveness model, as the end result of longstanding interactional difficulties.

### The Depressed Parent–Child Relationship

But what are the important characteristics of the parent–child relationship which may be blurred or omitted in a depressed family group? Lomas (1967) gives evidence from the experience of psychoanalysts and related disciplines for ways in which the family fails to provide the much needed psychological environment for its children through:

1. inadequate and unreliable affectionate fondling to satisfy the child's sensuous needs,
2. diminished ability to form accurate pictures of reality because of the confusing way it is presented to him by others,
3. dulling of the child's capacity to express and receive emotional experience by discouraging responses from others,
4. lack of clarity in the developmental path and an inadequate leader on which to model.

To consider these points in more detail we will first look at the material dealing with attachment by Bowlby (1958), Schaffer (1971) and others. Bowlby emphasizes 'monotropy' or attachment to one individual as being of primary importance, and Schaffer sees the object choice for attachment as depending on the individual's responsiveness to the infant's signals indicating a need for attention. This relates not only to the availability of the individual, but to the quality of their attentiveness and the intensity of their interaction with the infant. Thus an unstimulating mother could be rejected in preference for a very attentive father. The attachment figure needs to make the child feel secure and safe so that he/she is able to feel free to explore, to be adventurous and to grow through experience.

Bowlby (1958) has described six responses in the baby which lead to attachment behaviour and they are, crying, smiling, following, clinging, sucking and calling. The sensitivity with which mother and child are able to interact is all important in terms of their responsiveness to each other, the quality of their smiling and greeting responses and the warmth and enjoyment that they are able to communicate to each other during their physical contact and mutual awareness they show for each other's proximity. Adequate bonding leads to reliable affectionate handling and fondling which satisfies the child's sensuous needs. Later a dynamic equilibrium becomes established between the child's attachment and exploratory behaviour and the mother's caring and her other competing activities which take her away from the child. The mother who is quick to understand and respond to her child's needs provides a secure base from which he/she is able to grow, but if she is insensitive or unaware and withholds herself from this interaction then disturbance and insecurities arise. The young mother who is depressed may be affectively dulled and find it difficult to cope with the high level of emotional demand that a young child makes on her. Her repertoire of non-verbal responses such as her facial expression, use of smiling and looking may be diminished. She may find physical contact unfulfilling or even distasteful and resent her baby's needs for cuddling and holding. These factors reduce the intensity of her interaction with her baby, and may give rise to an irritable, crying, whining and dissatisfied infant who makes demands by other routes such as feeding difficulties, restlessness, delayed control of bowel and bladder function and separation difficulties. The mother for her part may become increasingly anxious and rejecting of her child's demands and at the same time experience a sense of guilt and fear about her handling of her child, which may lead to a controlling over-protective form of motherhood. These early patterns of feeling — expressed and covert — can set the patterns for future interaction throughout the child's lifetime.

Weismann and Paykel (1974) describe clearly in their study of depressed women the high levels of hostility they found in the intimate relationships of these women with their partners and children and the decreasing levels of hostility that was manifest in relationships of diminishing significance. They comment that the most withdrawn depressed patient in the interview situation can be extremely hostile in her home. She usually covers up this sort of behaviour because of her own ambivalence and sense of guilt and passes it off in socially acceptable terms by suggesting that she cannot tolerate her children's noise, thus avoiding any mention of her feeling of aggression towards them.

They described parenthood as one of the principal areas of role difficulty for the depressed woman. She was only moderately involved with her children's daily life and running into difficulties in her level of communication with them, expressing anxiety about an awareness of loss of feelings of affection and increased friction in her dealings with them. She tended to become hostile and over-protective or over-indulgent. There were commonly housework difficulties which were also indicative of another area where she had problems as a wife and mother. At the same time if she was engaged in outside work she coped more effectively with this. They agree with Brown (1975) that employment away from the family may serve a protective function and go some way to assist her in her own expression of personal and individual needs. They also found that her behaviour in relation to friends and relatives was characterized by 'discomfort, uneasiness and sensitivity' and it was increased where there were expectations for this sort of contact linked to the families' cultural background and social level. They found the most difficult periods in the life cycle to be infancy, adolescence and the empty nest era. The depressed woman was emotionally unavailable to her children and at the same time had problems within herself of autonomy and intimacy. The writers go on to suggest that later behaviour problems with her children stem from her own poor self-definition and self-understanding. She is excessively submissive and dependent compared with a sample of ordinary women, though still capable of domineering and manipulative behaviour. Therefore as an identity figure we can understand that the depressed woman presents a diffuse, poorly differentiated model vacillating weakly between ambivalent feelings of concern and rejection. She confuses her children's cognitive appraisal of reality and disturbs the formation of their own value systems. Thus in psychoanalytic terms the development of ego and superego becomes impaired and there are weak ego boundaries in the children.

This type of family system would fit into the lower end of Minuchin's (1974) continuum of family types which ranges from the enmeshed family system, where boundaries between members are poorly defined, to the other end of the continuum where family members disengage from each other by the formation of rigid boundaries. In the former group a sense of belonging to the family demands a major yielding of personal autonomy to the system and reduces any autonomous exploration or mastery of coginitive–affective skills. The depressed patient through a lack of personal autonomy and boundary differentiation generates anxieties and hostile dependencies in the family group. Feelings of potential loss lead to an inability in the developing child to form their own identity and any attempts to differentiate and move away from the family commitments may lead to an overwhelming sense of angry guilt and shame. It may be demonstrated by demanding tyrannical behaviour in the infant, rebellious deviant behaviour in the adolescent and guilt ridden conflicts about responsibilities in early adult life.

Bowlby (1975) discusses this same problem from the child's viewpoint and describes the pathological results of separation or threats to separation in childhood. Separation anxiety is the end of an ambivalent maternal influence. The conflict of rejection, guilt and over-protection lead in turn to a hostile, insecure and dependent child who continues to have major separation difficulties in childhood, adolescence or adult life. These difficulties may be expressed as school phobia or refusal, as an angry insecure regression in adolescence and as agoraphobic symptoms in adult life. Bowlby also emphasizes the conspiracy of denial which can be set up between mother and child in which they both shield the other from criticism or accusation and thereby perpetuate the situation.

## The Role of the Older Generation

But what of the previous generation and the part that they play in influencing disturbances within the family system? They have already exerted a major influence in shaping and forming some of the attitudes, ideas and prejudices which are being focused on the present difficulties. Grandparents have also produced models and styles for the handling of family disputes and may reinforce these old patterns by their present behaviour. The power which they exert within the family group will depend on a range of factors from geographical proximity to economic dependence and last but not least, the effectiveness of the emotional separation which has occurred between them and their grown child, as a result of maturation and the new attachment which marriage offers. If this has been an inadequate separation and has led to a fragile level of harmony and equilibrium in the new relationship, then any breakdown will immediately offer an opening for Granny or Grandpa to reasser her/his old influence within the relationship. If depression has emerged and there is an invitation to cherish and nurture then the opportunity presents for the older person to re-enter the scene in a possessive, rescuing sense. At the same time there is a message of helplessness and need being expressed coupled with an urge to regress to a childlike dependency which permits the full expression of old, well-learn patterns of communication and caring. As this dependency becomes reinforced so the marital partner becomes increasingly remote and alienated and if the reward continue then the opportunities to re-establish an open relationship diminish.

A case example will illustrate these changing patterns of alignment.

Mr. X had been an only child always very close to his parents and his mother had died the year he married. He wanted to offer his father a home and his new wife went along with the idea. The arrangement worked reasonably well for 15 years during which time they produced a son themselves. Then his father retired and became a permanent figure around the house and garden and this introduced a strain for his wife who increasingly resented her father-in-law for his presence in the home and the demands which he made on her husband for companionship. She expressed these frustrations through bitter, hostile and resentful outbursts and when she found little response from her husband began to develop new interests and friendships away from the home. The husband found his wife's demands impossible to meet and felt anxious and threatened within their precarious relationship. He became guilty and depressed and increasingly orientated towards his father to the extent that they became inseparable, sharing possessions and leisure hours together in the garden or the 'local'. He found comfort and reassurances within the old and much cherished father–son relationship and found another safer role for himself. Suddenly his father died leaving him bereft and lost and he turned to his wife for understanding and support, only to find that she was no longer emotionally available to him, had found a new strength for herself within her separate role, and had little motivation to redefine her position yet again. His difficulties were increased by the son leaving home at the same time.

## Patterns of Subsequent Disorder in the Next Generation

In all of these descriptions the difficulties are seen as longstanding ones operating throughout the child's critical years and leaving their heritage problems for the next generation of adults who in turn have major personal difficulties. Pre-existing marital conflicts are the key to mother child ambivalences and the relationship with the child becomes an important re-alignment for the mother and a further emotional support in her own life, and perhaps these will be clarified if we examine some exemplifying cases.

Miss D is a 20 year old girl who came complaining of feelings of depression and confusion and an inability to move away from her parents' home without becoming panicky and fearful. She expressed considerable resentment at the way her depression-prone mother had infantilized and over-protected her throughout her life and felt that she had hung on to her at all stages of her development. At the same time she was terrified of any possibility of losing her mother through holiday separation and had fears for her death in years to come. The pressures upon her to become independent were mounting as each year passed and she became increasingly demoralized and depressed herself, opting out on all fronts from the fields of endeavour she had previously found very challenging. There had been anxieties within her parents' marriage for many years and Miss D's mother commanded concern and interest through depressive episodes which tied her busy husband to her side. This was very clear too in the therapeutic relationship which the girl constructed in such a hostile dependent way that she finally changed therapists because she mistrusted the growing security of this more normal relationship.

Mistrust can also manifest itself by withdrawal, isolation, and an avoidance of situations and relationships which make a demand for intimacy and commitment. Repeated hospitalizations or frightening behaviour on the part of the depressed parent may make it unsafe for the children to expose their emotional needs or to make any attempts to form a close attachment. They may look for parental approval or disapproval as an important substitute and drive themselves to great achievements by continued industry and application at school or in the house or alternatively may 'malevolently' seek vociferous criticism and blame as their only route to acknowledgement and an expression of concern. This defensive withdrawal at a critical age may lead to major difficulties in later peer and sexual relationships, and this emergent pattern is well illustrated in the next case.

Mr. E, a young married man, came complaining that he could not communicate freely with his wife and that this had been the case throughout their courtship and engagement and the 15 months of their marriage. In fact, he indicated that he had had a similar experience with earlier girl friends and tended to make few friends at any time. When he was seven his parents separated and divorced after years of marital strife and he and his brother were sent to boarding school. He became a quiet, industrious self-sufficient little boy who did well academically, but grew up to feel he did not know his mother. As a result of the conflict and depression that her broken marriage had produced she disengaged herself from her family, taking up her previous career as a model and in her contacts with her son had expressed her feelings of ambivalence for him, continuing to confuse and threaten his sense of attachment to her by cajoling and criticizing him. He retained an infantile dependence for his mother's approval and concern and developed an inability to trust and feel secure in peer relationships and heterosexual contacts. He became isolated and depressed during his student years and after several unsuccessful relationships, married a girl who was potentially warm and comforting, but had her own problems of poor self-esteem and lack of confidence. In this setting he became acutely anxious and was troubled by poverty of ideas and thoughts when confronted by his wife. It soon became clear that this pattern of behaviour had a wilful rejecting element to it and became the only way that he expressed resentment and aggression when a demand was made for intimacy and closeness.

### Prime Disturbance in the Marital Relationship

Finally in this chapter we will focus on the characteristics of the depressed patients and spouses' behaviour which influences their capacity to relate to each other at an intimate and committed level. This can be partly illustrated from our own studies and although these are described in detail in Chapter 5 a brief outline of salient findings is in place here. In the sample of couples where one partner was being treated for depression as a psychiatric in-patient, high levels of tension and hostility appeared to be a major feature. We viewed this type of relationship arising as a result of the disturbance of individual responsiveness and the consequent production of feelings of uncertainty and insecurity within the relationship. This in its turn would lead to the interpersonal friction, hostility and resentment so well described and understood by depressed individuals. These feelings then increase the sense of fear and possible loss of the loved object and are followed by a wave of guilt and remorse which once more add fuel to the sense of anxiety and tension which have already been generated. Feelings of hostility do, however, generate an urge to withhold and become remote within the relationship as well as to increase the need to make an angry demand for reassurances.

In contrast, we were able to show the relaxed or mutually supportive behaviour of our control couples who used high levels of emotional expressiveness, but exhibited little tension or hostility and were able to confront each other with confidence and use conciliatory techniques such as agreement, laughter and joking when their arguments became too difficult. In a similarly detailed study but involving only normal married couples and their conflicts, Raush and coworkers (1974) found that resolving and reconciling became the most important tactics to ensure a continuing good relationship.

It becomes clear, then, that within the depressed couples' relationships the hostility and tension which is generated prevents the couple from confronting and negotiating with each other. Distance maintaining techniques such as Raush and his colleagues describe become the style for dealing with their differences. They found that husbands were more coercive dominant, used greater punitiveness and resorted to personal grievance and disparagement in their arguments. For their part wives tended to be more conciliatory, but did become locked in 'tit for tat' situations with their partners, or alternatively resorted to the changing roles of 'lamb and tiger' or victim and persecutor.

It is a feature of the depressed individual's behaviour to isolate him/herself from intimate contacts. This is done through a defensive technique of avoidance by an expression of hostility, irritation and open rejection. He or she becomes unavailable and exhibits prickly awkward behaviour and yet at the same time expresses his/her ambivalence in the situation by making a regressed dependent and childlike demand on their relatives. In a sense one might argue that they are testing the integrity of the family system by their repeated demands and conflicting messages. Unfortunately, as with any neurotic process, it is a self-defeating one and the individual sets up a situation where he/she experiences what he most fears, which is the criticism and rejection of the person he most values. The depressive message of self blame and punishment then becomes the final test of the situation and if this message does not meet with the desired response, can lead on to total withdrawal. It is at this point that delusional systems may arise where the ideas may involve most intimate relatives. The sense of despair and impending doom which drives them on to seek their own destruction may then include others. It is in this setting that extreme forms of self punishment may become generalized outwards to include grievous injuries towards their own family, and the depressed mother may starve or damage her child, or the father may see a need to exterminate himself and the rest of his family with him.

We have not so far considered the effects of these interactive difficulties on the sexual life of the married couple which are obviously of great importance. Loss of libido is classically considered to be one of the characteristics of the depressed patient and links up with the loss of feeling so often described for the sexual partner and family. Sexual behaviour is an integral part of the expression of affection between individuals. It also indicates a wish to be close and intimate within the relationship. The signal quality of depressive behaviour itself indicates the need to withdraw emotionally and this is expressed within the sexual act by withholding emotionally and physically. In the depressed female this is shown by lack of interest and a low level or absence of physiological responsiveness, which leads to vaginal dryness and some physical discomfort during intercourse, which in its turn further discourages and confirms her need to avoid the situation. Difficulty in achieving an orgasm also becomes a feature and the old pleasures seem to be unattainable. These observations were confirmed by Weissman and Paykel in their sample of depressed women and they demonstrated the increased submissiveness and dependency of their females who were reticent about their sexual problems and experienced considerable guilt and resentment about them. Their lack of assertiveness impaired their capacity to show affection.

A husband may indicate his withdrawal by indifference and apathy and erectile incompetence, which may further increase his anxiety in association with love-making and induce a progressive decline into impotence. In the older man this may pose a major problem if the situation if perpetuated for a long period, as although his ability to be intimate at an emotional level may return, his sexual competence may remain impaired. In some individuals the sexual act becomes repulsive and the avoidance can be complete. We can recall one patient who had experienced her sexual relationship as a very important aspect of her marriage, but when depressed became revolted by her husband's approaches and extremely anxious and fearful about his expectations of her. In such a situation the withholding can be so complete that a secondary vaginismus and frigidity becomes a feature. It is interesting to meet such sexually competent women who withhold from their husbands and also despise themselves for their behaviour and yet can become aroused and responsive within an extramarital relationship which they see as forbidden and sometimes degrading. They are able to function in a situation where there is no real emotional commitment involved and where they are deliberately flouting their husband's claim on them and yet at the same time find a masochistic pleasure in the sense of guilt and shame which the other relationship brings.

Sexual frustrations play an important part in feeding the sense of rejection and resentment and hostility already operating within the relationship and can become a problem area which engenders major anxieties and fears for the security of the marriage. It may strengthen alliances with the children to the extent that fathers may jealously guard the development of their daughters and mothers hang on to the dependent qualities of their sons. Once again the family system must absorb the stresses that the problem produces. Reticence and inhibition about sexual matters may once again become a poor identity model for the next generation. The young child may develop an acute awareness of a lack of any open expression of affection at a physical level between parents or between himself and parents. Anxieties and guilt about prohibitions for this sort of behaviour can become the family style.

## The Effect of Therapy on the Family

Finally in this chapter we look at the imposed or iatrongenic effects that therapists can contribute to the social consequences of disturbed family bonds. A long term admission to a mental hospital can mean that the family works through its sense of bereavement or loss in relation to the absent member and re-establishes a new equilibrium without that person. The children learn to turn to other parent substitutes or offer each other sibling support and take up new positions in relation to each other. When mother or father eventually returns home the family once again has to make new adjustment to admit the extruded family member once more to the family group. The older child may resent the parent's expectations that he or she will revert to the old style and patterns of behaviour and the younger child becomes confused about its primary attachments. In addition the absent parent may have major problems in re-establishing a valid role for themselves once again and this can in its turn produce further despair and depression in an already vulnerable personality. Perhaps the effects of drugs should also be mentioned. They do not affect the quality of a relationship, but the tranquillizing properties of some drugs can make the individual a slowed up, less responsive person who may communicate a sense of reduced sensitivity and involvement in relation to their children. It has recently been shown that the Diazepine group of tranquillizers can have a powerful disinhibiting effect in some individuals and can be responsible for aggressive behaviour within the family. It has also been suggested as one reason for the violent behaviour of family 'batterers'. The whole ethos of the mental hospital scene with its emphasis on conformity and the good patient image has its impact on the individual who has let go of her usual ties and commitments. Happily, ideas are changing now and we are increasingly seeing our patients returning home regularly at the weekends and retaining a greater sense of personal involvement with their spouse and their families. It is at all times of the utmost importance that we should look further than the immediate problems of symptoms of the patient who presents for treatment. The ripples do spread further within the family and produce their effects in other disturbed patterns of behaviour.

# 8

# COPING WITH CHANGE

This might seem a strange title for the last chapter of this book, but in fact we have been arguing that this is what depression is all about. Or rather, *not* about in the acute depressive phase, since people then are often most resistant to change. We have put forward the case for considering that depression is an experience both of the individual and of the couple which becomes an unsatisfactory way of trying to avoid the apparently more painful process of adaptation. We say 'apparently' because obviously depression itself can be such a painful experience that constructive change — although threatening — could certainly not be as painful. But the problem often appears to be that the depressive response defines the interpersonal situation, so that no other change then even appears possible.

Could it be that the world is now such a changeful place for Western urban industrialized man and woman that potential, and actual, psychological loss is just becoming impossible to deal with other than by psychopathological methods like depression? This has been seriously suggested by some writers although the base data is hard to interpret. Most of the known figures refer to the most severe cases of depression, often psychotic depression, and this category seems unlikely to have changed much over the last decades. But considerations of so-called 'neurotic' depression tend to show that there are increases in the incidence and certainly the clinical prevalence of these less severe kinds of depression. One of the striking changes seems to be that in the post-war period depression has become increasingly common in all decades of maturity, whereas previously it was thought to be largely found in the fifth decade and onwards.

Some workers have linked this increase to continuously rising levels of aspiration in all areas of life and thus the inevitability of disappointment and actual loss became greatly enhanced. In medical care the apparent 'miracles' of modern medicine have led to similar expectations which very frequently just cannot be met, so that apparent chronic sickness may well be the result of such medical care rather than the miracle cure which so many people imagine it to be. It could be that currently we are not very good at exposing growing children and young people to the emotional response to loss (particularly of personal relationships) which enables them to develop creative and reparative methods for coping with these difficulties. This is most certainly reflected in the rising tide of para-suicide which is reported over the last decade or so in all Western countries, and which may be a function of two myths about modern life — (1) that the emotional pain of stressful life events is unbearable and, (2) that medicine has the cure for such pain readily available in the freely prescribed psychotropic drugs. The combination of these two myths is becoming increasingly life-threatening. Perhaps one should add a third myth, which holds that all human relationships must be fruitful and satisfying — and certainly never boring and irritating.

Most writers that we have discussed in the previous chapters relate depression to loss or threatened loss of personal relationships and this is what we have been at pains to emphasize in our account as well. But we have argued it in a different way and have stood the usual reasoning on its head and said that, far from being the withdrawal from interpersonal life which many writers and clinicians have assumed it to be, we see depression as often an intensification of a relationship in an attempt by the depressed person to focus attention on their plight. This, then, highlights marriage as being the crucible for depression because of the intense psychological experiences which spouses often create for each other, and a number of writers have found a clear link between marriage and depression. One recent study by Levitt and Lubin (1975) has disputed this conclusion, and their evidence is culled from the responses to a nationwide sample survey in the U.S.A. This, however, must be somewhat suspect since it was not an epidemiological study of depression, but rather the inclusion of a depression scale with other survey material conducted by a national sampling agency. Further, they had no data on their non-married sample which identified them in terms of divorce or bereavement.

Perhaps we need to repeat once more that we certainly do not believe that the unmarried do not get depressed — to do so would be ludicrous — but that close and intimate relationships of the marital kind seem very frequently to be the setting for the disorder. It may well be true that our model of emotional ambivalence, poor self-esteem and subsequent meta-rules for rigid communication can apply to other close relationships as well, but that it seems to be particularly relevant to marriage.

It is also possible that it is the very form of modern marriage which has produced the increasing rates of depression. Certainly the radical critics have argued this way, and in particular because married *women* seem to be more vulnerable than their unmarried sisters to psychological disturbance. It is widely accepted that women exceed men in terms of depressive disorders — could it be that depression is the disorder par excellence of the modern pressure-cooker marriage? If this were the case, then the therapy would be both radical and simple — namely to abandon the marital relationship as we know it and substitute for it some emotionally less demanding and less potent form of attachment. At the moment (as we pointed out in Chapter 1), the depressed patient couples who come for help to clinics still mostly want to organize their lives within the traditional framework of marriage, and often want the interdependence to become more pronounced (but also more healthy), rather than less. And we also reproduced the marriage figures for Britain in the first chapter which demonstrate that although the divorce rate may be escalating, it appears that the vast bulk of those divorcing seek remarriage — and thus rapidly get back into the emotional pair-bond again.

As far as women are concerned Weissman and Klerman (1977) have debated this issue at some length in order to find an answer to the questions which are raised by the double rate of depression amongst women and we considered this briefly at the end of Chapter 2. They begin by establishing that the observation is a true one and not simply an artefact of some other factors such as women's greater ease in seeking help or their greater exposure to stress. Their explanation then ranges over genetics, physiology, developmental psychology, and role expectations of women. They conclude that changing role expectations may well be a very important factor in differentially affecting women, but that one solution is to enable men and women to work together on the conditions which may produce the depression-prone marriage. They write:

'These new role expectations may also create intrapsychic conflicts, particularly for those women involved in traditional family tasks but who also desire employment and recognition outside the family'

and again:

'Depressions may occur not when things are at their worst, but when there is a possibility of improvement, and a discrepancy between one's rising aspirations, and the likelihood of fulfilling these wishes.'

They make the further point that these are not short-term changes alone, but the result of more widespread social psychological events. No such widespread explanation exists for men because it appears that there is nothing to explain. This is clearly not the case as we have been at pains to point out. It is almost as if investigators believe that the explanation for the differential rates of depression between the sexes explains depression for both men and women. What we have suggested is that perhaps the situations which initially contribute most to the depressive response by men are likely to be connected with their work, which itself is intimately bound up with marriage and with their masculine self-esteem, but nevertheless separate from it. This means that a husband is likely to have two rather separate sources of self-esteem even though they are very intimately linked in the emotional sense with his marriage relationship.

This difference in source of self-esteem as between men and women may be important therapeutically, because the problems of role performance at work and at home can to a degree be separated for men whereas for most women the two are inextricably linked. Superficially it may appear that it is more demanding for a man to face again his work situation than it is for a woman to resume work in the home. But this may well only relate to the difference in initial anxiety about role performance which is quite likely to disappear rapidly. Then the successful resumption of his work role often has a highly beneficial effect on the role of husband/father as well.

There must be many other similar differences in the psychological situations of men and women but by and large they remain to be unravelled for men. Yet not quite. In the experimental study which we described in Chapter 4, we found sharp differences in the communicative behaviour of men and women patients which clears some of the ground. It seemed as if the men in that study adopted a more straightforward dependent and regressive role vis-à-vis their wives than their counterparts. The women were more passive–aggressive and ambivalent with their husbands. This suggests that the male psychopathology may be a good deal simpler than the female, and one important difference may be that there is no covert struggle for power, and thus the male need for nurturance is more straightforward.

## Moving Toward Depression—Changes in the Couple

Although we have studied the processes which alter when a couple are depressed, we have not directly studied the way in which couples become aware of pathological changes within their relationship. We know that couples vary enormously in their ability to be able to perceive what is happening to their relationship and some seem very sensitive to the earliest of changes. Others, even in the depths of a severe depression, find nothing to report about their relationship although to the observer the changes are obvious. This comment is important because it may be taken from our subsequent discussion that we believe that couples should always find it easy to identify the changes in their relationship. We do not believe this to be so, but it may well prove very useful to identify the subtle changes which subsequently lead to pathological change and then to use these therapeutically with a couple at risk.

In our studies we have confirmed what others have noted, that in the setting of depression, people become much more pre-occupied with themselves. Their language betrays this preoccupation by their repeated use of personal pronouns. In any particular relationship, this may well be acknowledged when one partner says of the other, that they are becoming more selfish and self-centred. The expression 'selfish' will frequently be used in a pejorative way and this only serves to make the marital situation more difficult. Just as the individuals appear to be more preoccupied with themselves, so in depression the couple become preoccupied with the nature and quality of *their* relationship. It is common to discover in the stories of younger people who have eventually sought professional help with their depression, that they have previously turned to sensitivity groups and marriage enrichment courses in order to put right what they felt was wrong with their marriage.

Another feature of our study was that we noted the way in which the wife of a depressed couple became more controlling. This control took a number of forms but showed itself quite clearly in the style of language which she used. It is unlikely that the wife would notice this in herself; the husband may in the early stages notice that a change has taken place and may object to it. Other writers have commented on the way in which some of the very early signs of depression include minimal withdrawal from social interchange. Our observations tend to support this to the extent that the controlling devices which the wife uses can easily be extended to a social withdrawal. Although we have no research evidence directly linking these aspects of depression together, clinically they do seem to be linked, at least for some patients.

The kind of processes which we are attempting to describe can find expression in many aspects of a couple's relationship. They are not limited to verbal exchanges, but also can be found in non-verbal aspects of their communication.

We have also noted how the depressed couple's pattern of behaviour and style of communication becomes increasingly rigid and rule-governed and yet it is capable of relaxing and becoming easier and more flexible by the end of treatment. The rigidity of the rules is something which is experienced by each of the partners, but which is rarely commented on. Occasionally we have had patients who have commented on the spontaneity and flexibility of their previous relationship when they were not depressed. The lack of these characteristics in their depressed life is their way of experiencing the new rules. Another way in which the new rigid rules can manifest themselves is by the couple becoming increasingly separate and mistrustful of each other. Couples can often be helped to be aware of this aspect of the change in their relationship and then discuss these difficulties of being open and trusting with their partners. At the same time the clinician must help them to appreciate the need for both of them to take the risk of exposing themselves to hurt and disappointment by trusting their partner once again in order to re-establish their old relationship. However, trust by one partner leaves the relationship unbalanced and at risk of further deterioration.

Perhaps one of the clearest signs of an early shift in the marriage in the direction of depression is seen when a couple resort to a testing and provocative pattern of gamesmanship. Unless they are aware of their motives they find themselves heading rapidly for the inevitable impasse which leads to frustration and dissatisfaction for both of them. One common example is the increasingly irritable wife who becomes much more strident and nagging in her attitude to her husband, so that he responds by withdrawal perhaps to the local public house, where he takes up again associations which have served to support him in the past — simply intensifying her feeling. Couples are often aware of the repetitive nature of these forms of behaviour and are distressed not only by being involved in them but also by the knowledge that they mostly end by leaving both of them miserable and estranged. The inevitability gives birth to and sustains hopelessness.

For the couple who are caught up in the processes of change and are aware that their marriage is altering under these pressures, there are a number of strategies which they can be helped to employ to alter the course of events. We have already intimated that the first and essential step which any couple can take is to recognize what is happening. Whether the couple make this discovery for themselves, or through the help of others, the steps which are open to them begin from this recognition. It may well be for certain couples that a pre-existing rigidity in their pattern of interaction prejudices their chances of taking this step and puts them most severely at risk at times of cirsis and change. .

The couple must be able to agree on any further course of action to avoid a further deterioration in their relationship. Any strategy needs to be invested by each of the partners with sufficient individual commitment for them each to be able to recognize and be convinced of the intentions of the other. A very common trap, after the mutual recognition of a problem, is for the couple to decide to do something which although in the right direction requires too many mutual steps for its easy completion. For example, a couple may recognize that their interests and activities over a period of years have led them to live almost entirely separate lives, and that in the absence of their children, the point of their living together has largely disappeared. They may decide that the solution to their particular problem is to find again a common interest and for them to spend more time together. These two aspects of their solution, 'more time together' and 'a common interest', both require enormous efforts on each of their parts in order to bring them about. The common interests can only emerge from a willingness to share ideas, and aspirations, as well as time. A more realistic goal would be for each of them to free enough time so that they might accomplish some small mutual task together rather than setting themselves impossible objectives. It might of course be that out of their recognition of the difficulties through which they are living, they would be able to use their new free time to seek help from some other person.

The sharing of an ultimate common goal may serve a useful purpose as we have suggested already, in assisting the couple to pool their resources and see themselves working together and sharing the responsibilities for the final outcome. Establishing a goal at the time of crisis may be therapeutic in forming a joint focus for their individual needs and energies. It may provide a structure on which they can build trust and prove their commitment to negotiation and mutual understanding.

We have drawn attention above to the fact that the major changes and crises which occur in the life of a married couple are those which tend to make the couple more isolated in society. Frequently, these crises also isolate the individuals within their marriage. A sense of loneliness and isolation plays a very important part in depression. It is obvious that the strategies devised by the couple which enhance their relationship with other people, are likely to be in the direction of health rather than depression. We believe that in general relationships with others outside the marriage, particularly if they are relationships which are shared by both members of the partnership, sustain the marriage rather than detract from it. This comes about by the couple being able to use other relationships as reference points for understanding their own roles in marriage. It also enables them to take outside the marriage some of their ideas and behaviour which cause them distress and to modify them in the light of their experience of both seeing other marriages in action and also talking with people about their own particular situation.

## Change and the Wider Context

In two chapters in the book there has been a discussion of the broader changes in people's lives which act historically and contemporarily on the depressed person and the spouse. They are the so-called predisposing factors which lead to the formation of the emotional response to loss or threat which eventually becomes identified as depression. Some of these factors lie back in the personal history of the individual and are therefore unalterable. Perhaps in terms of mental health more attention needs to be paid to experiences in childhood which produce sharp loss of self-esteem and the helpless and hopeless self-picture which results. All too frequently the effect of the loss-producing event on the child is not evident because the child's response is to 'go quiet' and therefore not be attended to. At least we now recognize that hospitalization and other separation experiences can have this effect, but our sensitivity needs to be much wider. One factor which is frequently cited in retrospective studies of depressed patients is that of bereavement in childhood. This suggests that many adults handle this change very badly for their children and leave them very vulnerable. It is still the case that children are too protected from the experience of bereavement in a misplaced concern for their current emotional well-being, when what they need is the help to deal with it, not to escape *from* it.

These and other experiences may nevertheless leave their mark and then the adult is vulnerable to later life stress. Depression which leads people to seek professional help rarely, if ever, occurs 'out of the blue', without it being possible for causal events to be clearly identified. There is now a large literature which deals with the way in which people attempt to cope with the crises which occur in their lives, and how one form of attempt to cope can, in fact, take the form of a clinical depression. There are also a number of studies, some of which we have quoted, which show that the individual's marital adaptation to a chronic neurotic disability of their partner, can also take the form of depression. These observations, which are in keeping with our own experience in the clinical field, have led us to consider ways in which it may be possible to anticipate change so that the full clinical picture of depression can be avoided. If we are right in what we have said about the emergent quality of depression arising from within the marital interaction, together with the evidence that we have on the effect of crises on the lives of individuals, then it should be possible for us to delineate with some clarity ways of avoiding the more severe aspects of depression. This is particularly likely to be true if we bear in mind the various characteristics of the marriages which seem to be predisposed to depression.

We would agree with Gerald Kaplan, who has argued in a number of works, that it is possible to identify crises which lead to psychological disorder in the lives of those who are involved. He has demonstrated that it is possible to organize in society, at a neighbourhood level, various agents who can be seen as resource people and who are available to others at risk in times of cirsis. These resource people come from a variety of backgrounds, including professional workers, such as psychologists, social workers, medical personnel and the clergy. In addition to this professional network, it is possible also to organize a network of voluntary helpers who are aware of the importance of recognizing a crisis and the possible consequence which may stem from it.

Holmes and Rahe (1967) have identified crises and rated them according to their potency for producing disorders. At the top of this list they place such events as bereavement and marital breakdown and descend through such traumatic happenings as imprisonment of family members, serious physical illness, lengthy unemployment, retirement through to minor every day occurrences. The characteristic of these crises is that they disrupt relationships. Most often they produce either a real, or imagined sense of isolation and they often redefine relationships in a way which leaves the person in crisis disadvantaged.

The importance of these observations is obvious as it enables the resource person, or would be helper, after recognizing a particular crisis, to be in a position to act in a way which may mitigate some of its more serious effects. Knowledge of the importance of the various crises in general is only a guide to knowing what the effects might be in any particular circumstances but, nevertheless, such lists are valuable in pointing to those events which are most likely to be associated with the development of disorders like depression.

Whether or not a helper may be able to intervene effectively depends almost entirely on that helper being able to establish an appropriate kind of relationship with the couple who are passing through the crisis. There is no doubt that couples who do not actively seek help, may be prepared to accept it when it is offered in the right way. This active prevention may well appear a luxury to those who work in services which are hard-pressed with large numbers of already sick patients. However, it has been demonstrated that it is possible to develop within a community a network of lay helpers who would actively intervene without the involvement of the professional services. There are now many examples in Western countries of lay groups who, because of their own experience of living through a particular crisis, have organized themselves to help others who have a similar problem. There are groups which deal with divorce, bereavement and in particular the bereavement through loss of a child. Through their own experience they are often very sensitive to the needs of those whom they would help and their initial approaches are not likely to be aggressively intrusive or impertinent, but they may exhibit skill and sophistication in handling the sufferer. They claim to offer to people in crisis what they often cannot produce from their own resources, or at times often do not perceive that they need. Their most valuable contribution is their empathy and a belief that life can continue.

When we talk about the strategies which a couple might resort to in order to cope more adequately with various crisis-producing changes, we run the risk of writing something which may appear as either trite or of the same genre as the syndicated 'advice columns' which appear in weekly magazines. However, we are certain that both from our research work and the work of many others, we now have a sufficiently firm basis from which we can write with some confidence. We in no way believe that we are writing the equivalent of a kind of journalistic 'happiness pill'. Rather, we write in the belief that there are things which couples can think and do together which have a real bearing on the likelihood of them coping adequately or not with change.

In Chapter 3 we discussed 'at risk' and 'vulnerability' factors which predispose to depression within a marriage. Although the individual may view these as 'givens' within their own personal problem area and thereby with some knowledge of their importance feel ever more hopeless about dealing with their difficulties, nevertheless understanding and awareness go a long way towards acceptance and motivation for change. In particular where marital partners are concerned, knowledge can heighten the patience and understanding and tolerance shown within the relationship at times of stress. Support and acceptance for changed patterns of behaviour with the expectation that their partner will alter yet again at a later date, are of crucial importance for tolerating major relationship and role shifts. Our own study indicated clearly how tensions, anxieties and insecurities influenced the spouse's pattern of response so that they might oscillate from a caring over-protective role to a rejecting misunderstood one.

There are many authors who have written at length about the styles which can be identified in various marriages. Of particular interest to us have been our observations on trust and lack of trust, communication patterns and control strategies within the marriage. Although these are fairly readily recognizable by an observer, it is far more difficult for the participants to be aware of the style which they characteristically pursue. Nevertheless it is quite clear clinically, that many couples who get into difficulties are aware that their relationship has been such as to leave them vulnerable at a time of crisis. However, a couple may construe this to themselves, it seems clear that to make this explicit between them, can be a step towards producing a change in their relationship style.

Many of the changes which are associated with depression can be anticipated. Bereavement, change of housing, loss of a job and many other changes are part of the usual expected course of events and can be seen some way ahead. In particular, that most pathogenic of changes, bereavement, can be anticipated more often than not. It has been shown both experimentally and in the study of clinical problems, such as the terminal illness of children with leukemia, that by rehearsing the bereavement or some other anticipated change, the degree of disruption at the time of the event can be lessened.

These experiments show that the level of distress engendered by the rehearsal must not reach the proportions of fear, otherwise the preparation may be counter-productive. Hence, it would seem that couples who are attempting to think ahead and look at some of the harsh realities of life, need to do this in such a way that it does not become either a major preoccupation for them, or distressful to the extent of being disruptive to their lives at a time when they are planning for, rather than experiencing, a crisis.

One of the positive things which a couple can do in order to live successfully through a crisis without it becoming a pathogenic experience, is to have a mutually agreed goal which is clearly beyond the time of the change. The goal may be a simple one or extend into the world of fantasy, but as long as it has some purchase on the style and function of the day-to-day life of the couple then it can provide a very important internal stabilizing and sustaining factor.

In the setting of change, couples are faced with at least two problems. One is the problem of recognizing the fact of the change and the other is identifying the alterations which are going on within the marital relationship. This is often very much more difficult for those directly involved in the change than for observers. For example, a couple whose teenage children are leaving home and establishing themselves independently from their parents, can within a few months move from living in a bustling busy household to one which is reduced to the father and mother alone. The change has taken place and suddenly things are different. Our every day experience confirms, what we meet clinically week by week, in the stories which our patients tell us, that such changes often take the couple by surprise.

This may seem surprising as there is no doubt that the well adjusted provident couple do anticipate change and rehearse their strategies to advance and where there is close understanding and trust can support each other through the difficult hiatus which appears. However, where communication and trust are a problem, no genuine strategy can be formulated and the couple approach new disasters with an inconsequential vacuousness which leads them to act impulsively, making excessive demands on a poorly defined relationship at these times of stress.

## Some Concluding Remarks

So far in this final chapter we have been drawing attention to some of the factors which seem to stem from our analysis. Although the evidence is by no means complete (and will probably never be) there is much to be said for perceiving depression in the new framework presented here, as an experience which is particularly felt by one person but in which very many of the important aspects can only be understood by reference to the depressed person's experience with an intimate other.

The problem of change is pervasive in all nature, and in some ways it is one of the marks of the human approach to life that people try to preserve and protect themselves from the restless surge of the external world. Yet it is natural in all species for there to be times when the individual withdraws from his world into himself in order to integrate experience, or to insulate himself from too demanding an environment. There is a curious paradox here which has not been considered in any great detail, that withdrawal can be, and often is, a proper strategy for marshalling resources and yet, taken to excess, it may actually prove irreversible. By the time this stage is reached, the biological substratum of withdrawal may be the most important level of organization to be considered, but most depressed people never reach this level and it is total nonsense to suggest that this is the proper level of understanding for all depression. What we have emphasized is that because of intimate social role structures, the message properties of the withdrawn depressed person are far greater than we usually admit — and that this may be a very important part of the depressive behaviour.

It is as the troubled person makes strenuous efforts to slow down and back off that the ordinary responsiveness of the intimate other becomes challenged and sometimes negated. Certainly every mental health practitioner knows that there is little to be gained by redoubling the exercise of one's ordinary interpersonal behaviour now, because it is against this that the depressed person is so often reacting, and often with considerable hostility. Sometimes in-patient treatment works precisely because the therapists no longer bother to respond to the power of the depressed message — which then forces the patient to behave in some other way in order to communicate their needs.

Our suggestions of systematic role analysis in these pathological situations (which we have illustrated with many examples) seem to offer a new and powerful approach to some of these problems and, as we have suggested earlier in the chapter, this same analysis may have preventive importance as well as therapeutic value. Certainly the evidence now accumulating is that pathological depression is a major problem which requires much effort and time devoted to increasing understanding and effective care.

Seligman (1975) has suggested that depression is the 'common cold' of psychopathology and this evocative phrase indicates its widespread nature. It underestimates the suffering and damage since it suggests that, although widespread, we need not worry too much about effective treatment since it is mostly self-limiting. This view has actually often been put forward, but the truth is that we do not really know the extent of the long-term effects of pathological depression, either on the individual or on the intimate social network. The most serious risk is obviously that of suicide, but it may be that we have overlooked more widespread problems of mental health in our anxiety to prevent the ultimate disaster occurring. It is not even clear that the bulk of people who commit suicide *are* depressed, and certainly suicide is equally common in a number of other pathological states (see Levitt and Lubin 1975). In Great Britain, at least, suicide appears to be slightly decreasing as a problem over the past few years.

What we have suggested earlier is that only within the community can adequate help be available to deal with the size of the problem and offer help to the individuals and families concerned. At the moment, perhaps, this help will be early attention to prevent a depressive system becoming established too firmly, but there is also the possibility that we should be paying much more attention to the precursors of depression in earlier family experiences. Social change is really not within the sphere of influence of individual workers, but there are other small-scale social processes which are in homes, in schools, and in work places. We hope that our emphasis on the most important of these — marriage and family — will give others a stimulus to look at the possibilities which exist for them of developing more effective work at every level to help suffering families and individuals as they struggle with this age-old human condition.

# APPENDIX

## MODELS AND METAPHORS OF DEPRESSION

The conceptual models which have been used in the past and up until the present time, are powerful linguistic devices which for two very good reasons have constrained our thinking about depression in such a manner that we think of depression only in terms of the individual and his body. The first constraint is intrinsic in the psychology of the metaphor. Both Koestler (1949) and Black (1962) see the metaphor, and hence the conceptual model, as very compelling in human experience, largely because its emotional component gives momentum to our thoughts and gives us great satisfaction when we feel we have used it appropriately. In the clinical situation this means that the model would not only determine which observations we made and the emphasis we placed on them, but would also lead to a sense of satisfaction when we believed that we had made sense out of the signs and symptoms offered by a depressed patient. It is unlikely that we would easily relinquish a tool which had served us well.

The second constraint to our thinking is the well-recognized pattern — to which scientists seem particularly prone — of taking a metaphor and reifying it. This means that an idea which has served happily as part of a metaphor eventually comes to indicate a discrete part of actual reality, that is to say to be regarded as substantive rather than metaphorical. Sarbin (1964, 1968 and 1969) has demonstrated that this is what has happened to the notion of anxiety, and Roberts (1973) has traced in detail the story for depression. Both anxiety and depression are today regarded as conditions in their own right. Yet depression started its life in medical writings when used in phrases like 'depression of spirits' and this continued for a considerable time. The change from metaphor actually began at about the turn of the century and the process of reification was virtually completed within ten years. Sarbin points out that a concept which is reified loses its 'as if' quality and is endowed with a concreteness and substance of its own which he argues is mythical. By now it has become a belief, and like all other beliefs, it is resistant to attack because it is strongly defended emotionally. It is interesting here to note that this process of reification is observable in other branches of science and Hinde (1965), Turner (1967) and Mainz (1971) all write of their own fields describing a similar pattern of development of ideas.

The next stage in our understanding is to try and grasp the ways in which the observer has grappled with the complex phenomena which go to make up depression. The word 'model' best expresses the clusters of explanation which have been used for this purpose and this can apply both to the older metaphorical understanding as well as to the more recent reified metaphor.

Over the centuries the two main models have been the metaphysical and the medical. The first has not found a place in the scientific approach since it uses astrological and mystical terms to create a model of depressive phenomena as part of vast processes in the cosmos. It is actually very much alive and the astrological charts and Tarot cards bear witness to this. The second group of models are those which can be called person-based medical models which explain that the process exists in the person in some way. It is this set of ideas which enables the individual to say that he has 'got' depression and allows the observer to think about how this should be according to his own predilection. The model springs from the theory rather than the reverse, and it therefore makes it possible to identify a limited number of models underlying a much larger number of theories. But a word of caution needs to be inserted here. In recent years the term 'medical model' has become widespread and often used by critics of medicine as almost a term of abuse. Here we are not judging the models as such, but simply saying that when depression is regarded as a disturbance or disorder rather than a visitation, the explanatory models have naturally been medical ones.

The first of these personal medical models is perhaps the most ancient and certainly one of the most pervasive and has its origins in the medicine and philosophy of Ancient Greece. This is the *humoural model* which construes the experience and behaviour of a depressed person as arising out of the movement and particular distribution of the life-sustaining substances, or humours, in the body. An early theory using this model and which persisted for many centuries was that depression or melancholia was related to the production and distribution of black bile and that this resulted in the observed behaviour. The modern humourists are, of course, the biochemists who use extremely sophisticated language and complex theories, but whose basic model is still the same. Despite the complex language, this quotation from Shopsin and Kline (1975) gives the clear flavour of the model. They write:

> 'The current biological theories of mania and depression are united in postulating a role for brain monoamines in this group of disorders ... [these theories] simply stated relate a functional deficit of brain neurotransmitter amines at specific central synapses in depression, and conversely, a functional excess of these amines in mania.'

The second (and equally ancient) model localizes the causes of depression in solid parts of the person and particularly in various parts of the brain. We shall call this type of model *solidist* and up until recently it was the neurophysiologists and neurosurgeons who espoused it most clearly. Freeman (1950) argued that it was clearly apparent that neurosis and psychosis both had their origin in the most anterior part of the frontal lobe.

Recent workers have been at some pains to indicate that they recognize more complex organizational features of the nervous system but even so, their writings often betray their use of the solidist model as they identify a part of the brain as the seat of the depression. For example, Knight (1969), when writing about the surgical treatment of depression, says:

'The surgical treatment of mental illness may be regarded as the surgery of the emotions. Since primitive emotions are damaging emotions in psychiatry, it may well be concluded that the isolation of primitive cortical areas would be significant in contributing to the results achieved.'

In the last resort both the humoural and solidist models are unsatisfactory because they do not allow consideration of a whole range of observations which do not fall into the area of either alone. But the two models have been combined more satisfactorily into a *constitutional* model. The basic idea here is that the form and development of the body determines the likelihood or otherwise of the individual to develop depression, and that physical constituents of the body, in particular the genes, govern the biochemical mechanisms of the body. A good modern example of those who rely on the constitutional model is Winokur and his colleagues (1969), who attempt to make the link between genetic factors, other biological factors and various kinds of depressive disorder.

The next model is much more sophisticated and in fact has to be differentiated into four different sub-forms. The general form we shall call the *organizational* model, in which depression is viewed as being the product of a whole series of interrelated events which may well be occurring at different levels of the organization. This model is used by a whole range of disciplines which have been interested in depression from neurophysiology through to psychoanalysis and it is by far the most important and extensively applied model which is in use today. Von Bertalanffy (1974) refers to it as the 'robot' or 'zoomorphic' model of man and says:

'This conception was common to all major schools of American psychology, classical and neobehaviourism, learning and motivation theories, psychoanalysis, cybernetics, the concept of the brain as a computer, and so forth.'

The four sub-forms of the model have been very clearly identified by Rapaport (1960) in his work on psychoanalytic theory and we shall use his notation here. The first of these sub-forms is one which has been important in theories of motivation and which is often couched in hydrodynamic terms. The model uses the general notion of behaviour resulting from the direction and magnitude of pressures within the mind, and uses terms like tension release, overflow, pressure, stream and so on. Failure to relieve pressure is one of the cardinal pathological ideas in the causation of disturbed behaviour. It is called the *entropy* or *economic* sub-model for reasons obviously connected with the notion of flow and tension.

In psychoanalytic thought this sub-model views depression as the result of the direction of psychic energy against the self in the form of aggressive or angry feelings, the depression arising out of the way in which these feelings are processed. Freud and later similar writers who have drawn attention to the link between anger and depression, are reiterating and reformulating the model which has been clearly expounded down the centuries. St. Thomas Aquinas (c. 1250) wrote vividly of the link between fear, anger and sorrow (depression):

> 'Nevertheless fear and anger cause great harm to the body by reason of the sorrow which they imply ...
> ... because a hurtful thing hurts yet more if we keep it shut up because the soul is more intent on it, whereas if it be allowed to escape the soul's intention is dispersed, as it were, on outward things, so the inward sorrow (depression) is lessened.'

By his use of the phrase 'as it were' St. Thomas is clearly aware that his model is certainly not to be reified! Freud developed his own model in a different way and writes (Freud, 1917):

> 'In grief we found the ego's inhibited condition and loss of interest was fully accounted for by the absorbing work of mourning. The unknown loss in melancholia would also result in an inner labour of the same kind and hence would be responsible for the melancholic inhibition.'

Despite the different language and the gap of hundreds of years the central metaphor is remarkably similar.

The second sub-model is the *topographic* one which tries to locate in some structure the stimulus which leads to the depressive response. In behaviourist theories the stimulus is located outside the individual whereas in psychoanalytic thought the stimulus is located both outside, (in terms of loss) and inside in terms of anxious guilt arising from within and to which depression is the ultimate response.

The idea which is fundamental to the third sub-model is that an individual must pass through a series of psychological and/or physical stages in order to reach a certain end-point. Freud (1917) makes this quite clear in discussing his view of depression, when he says that the depressed person, in his view, is using the psychological mechanisms appropriate to the oral phase of development. This model is named the *Darwinian* model and again for obvious reasons. It is clearly similar to the major *constitutional* model we have discussed above, but does not imply physical structure. Many other writers use this explanatory model without using the complex intrapsychic structure of Freud.

A good example of this similar alternative approach is that of Beck (1967) who writes of the way in which the individual's history will determine the likelihood of his developing depressive responses. He sees the growing young person becoming sensitized to certain types of life situation which 'embed' the negative attitudes that comprise what he calls the 'depressive constellation' which builds up as part of the develodevelopmental process. It follows that Beck's treatment within this model is to expose and eradicate these well-established thought patterns.

The last of the organizational sub-models is concerned with the hierarchical organization of the psychological factors. This implies that higher levels in the hierarchy order those levels below. The prime hierarchy in the psychoanalytic formulation is that of unconscious, preconscious, and conscious with the interposed structures of id, ego, and superego, and this has obvious connections with other types of model. Rapaport suggests that the name of *hierarchical* model is applied to this formulation to suggest the part which level plays in ordering the level beneath it, but also determining some of the activities of the level above. This is clearly used by the psychoanalysts when they propose that the role of the superego in depression is to try and control and punish the ego in an exaggerated and overbearing way.

These four sub-models can be teased out in the way which we have done here, but they are also used in combination with each other in more complex arrangements. Two recent writers have recently done this to propose rather different models within the larger organizational model. The first of these is Seligman (1975) whose theory of learned helplessness is an important contribution. Here we need to emphasize the organizational model at the base of the theory which includes aspects of the hierarchical, Darwinian and topographic sub-models in its formulation. The actual depressed experience is certainly hierarchical in the sense that a powerful response of helplessness effectively prevents other, more healthy responses when the person is faced with a painful situation. Akiskal and Mckinney (1975) actually embrace Seligman's theory in their synthesis of a round dozen theories of depression. They propose a hierarchical model for all the theories with certain neurophysiological brain systems as being the superordinate level. This is probably an impossible task since this approach ultimately needs a fusion of the *organizational* and *solidist* models — which is probably just not logically possible.

The reader will have been aware that as we moved through this discussion of models our account has had to become more and more complex. Yet not one of the models really takes into account to any significant degree the interaction of the depressed person with another person. This in fact points to the major deficiency of the personal medical models which is that people are seen — if at all — as stimuli or reinforcers.

We are particularly concerned about this latter point. We believe that it exemplifies the major deficiency of the medical model as a whole. Patients are seen as having conditions which are nothing but abnormalities in this or that system, or in part of the brain, or in one psychic function or another. The total reductionism of this view of man, which is largely determined by the medical model, leads us to search for a more adequate model which would enable us to incorporate what we know about ourselves and other observations which were not encompassable by the medical models.

# References

Ackerman, N. W. (1958). *The Psychodynamics of Family Life*, New York, Basic Books Inc.
Akiskal, H. S. and McKinney, W. T. (1975). 'Overview of recent research in depression', *Archives of General Psychiatry*, **32**, 285–305.
Anonymous (1975). 'Depressive illness: A shared experience', *Marriage Guidance*, **15**, No. 7, 251–256.
Aquinas, St. Thomas. *Summa Theologican* (1914 Ed.), London, B. and I. Washbourne Ltd.
Arieti, S. (1974). Affective disorders; manic-depressive psychosis and psychotic depression — manifest symptomatology, psychodynamics, sociological factors, and psychotherapy. In S. Arieti (Ed.) *American Handbook of Psychiatry*, Vol. 3, 2nd Ed, New York, Basic Books.
Ayd, F. J. (1961). *Recognising the Depressed Patient*. New York, Grune and Stratton.
Bales, R. F. (1951). *Interaction Process Analysis*. Reading, Mass., Addison-Wesley.
Barry, W. A. (1970). 'Marriage research and conflict: an integrative review', *Psychological Bulletin*, **73**, 41–54.
Bateson, G. (1973). *Steps to an Ecology of Mind*. St. Albans, Paladin.
Beck, A. T. (1967). *Depression; Clinical, Experimental and Theoretical aspects*. New York, Hoeber.
Berne, E. (1964). *Games People Play*. London, Penguin.
Bertalanffy, L. von (1968). *General Systems Theory*. New York, Braziller.
Biddle, B. J. and Thomas, E. J. (Eds.) (1966). *Role Theory; Concepts and Research*. New York, Wiley.
Black, M. (1962). *Models and Metaphors*. Ithaca, New York, Cornell U.P.
Blood, R. O. and Wolfe, D. M. (1960). *Husbands and Wives: The Dynamics of Married Living*. London, Collier–MacMillan.
Blumenthal, M. D. and Dielman, T. E. (1975). 'Depressive symptomatology and role function in a general population', *Archives of General Psychiatry*, **32**, 985–991.
Boszormenyi-Nagy, I. and Sparks, G. (1973). *Invisible Loyalties*. New York, Harper and Row Inc.
Bowlby, J. (1925). *Attachment and Loss 1. Attachment*. London, Penguin Books.
Bowlby, J. (1975). *Attachment and Loss 11. Separation: Anxiety and Anger*. London, Penguin Books.
Bowlby, J. (1977) 'The Making and Breaking of Affectional Bonds: I Aetiology and Psychopathology in the Light of Attachment Theory'. *British Journal of Psychiatry*, **130**, 201–210.
Brim, O. G. (1958). 'Family structure and sex-role learning by children', *Sociometry*, **XXI**, 1–16.
Briscoe, C. W. and Smith, J. B. (1973). 'Depression and marital turmoil', *Archives of General Psychiatry*, **29**, 811–817.
Brown, G. W., Harris, T. O., and Peto, J. (1973). 'Life events and psychiatric disorder: 2 Nature of causal link', *Psychological Medicine*, **3**, 159–176.

Brown, G. W., Bhrolchain, M. N., and Harris, T. (1975). 'Social class and psychiatric disturbance among women in an urban population', *Sociology*, **9**, 225–254.

Brown, G. W., Harris, T., and Copeland, J. (1977). 'Depression and loss', *British Journal of Psychiatry*, **130**, 1–18.

Cadoret, R. J. (1972). 'Depressive disease: life events and onset of illness', *Archives of General Psychiatry*, **26**, 133–136.

Cameron, N. (1963). *Personality Development and Psychopathology*. Boston, Houghton Mifflin.

Charney, E. J. (1966). 'Psychosomatic manifestations of rapport', *Psychotherapy Systems and Psychosomatics*, **28**, No. 4.

Chester, R. (1971). 'Health and marriage breakdown: Experience of a sample of divorced women', *British Journal of Preventive Social Medicine*, **25**, 231–235.

Clare, A. (1976). *Psychiatry in Dissent*. London, Tavistock Publications.

Collins, J., Kreitman, N., Nelson, B., and Troop, J. (1971). 'Neurosis and marital interaction III. Family roles and functions', *British Journal of Psychiatry*, **119**, 233–242.

Costello, C. G. (1972). 'Depression: loss of reinforcers or loss of reinforcers effectiveness', *Behaviour Therapy*, **3**, 240–247.

Covi, L., Lipman, R. S., and Derogatis, L. (1973). 'Imipramine, diazepam and group psychotherapy in long term treatment of depressive neurosis', *Psychopharmacology Bulletin*, **9**, 57–59.

Coyne, J. C. (1976). 'Depression and the response of others', *Journal of Abnormal Psychology*, **85**, 186–193.

Coyne, J. C. (1976). 'Toward an interactional description of depression', *Psychiatry*, **39**, 28–40.

Crago, M. (1972). 'Psychopathology in married couples', *Psychological Bulletin*, **77**, 114–128.

Crawford, M. P. (1972). 'Retirement and role-playing', *Sociology*, **6**, 217–236.

Crown, S. (1976). Marital breakdown, epidemiology and psychotherapy. K. Granville-Grossman (Ed.) *Recent Advances in Clinical Psychiatry No. 2*. Edinburgh, Churchill Livingstone.

Dalton, K. (1971). 'Prospective study into puerperal depression', *British Journal of Psychiatry*, **118**, 689–692.

Davidson, P. O. (Ed.) (1976). *The Behavioural Management of Anxiety Depression and Pain*. New York, Brunner–Mazel.

Davis, D. Russell (1970). 'Depression as adaptation to crisis', *British Journal of Medical Psychology*, **43**, 109–116.

Dicks, H. V. (1967). *Marital Tensions*. London, Routledge and Kegan Paul.

Dominion, J. (1972). 'Marital pathology: A review', *Postgraduate Medical Journal*, **48**, 517–525.

Eisenstein, V. W. (Ed.) (1956). *Neurotic Interaction in Marriage*. London, Tavistock Publications.

Eisler, R. M. and Polak, P. R. (9173). 'Social stress and psychiatric disorder', *Journal of Nervous and Mental Disease*, **153**, 227–233.

Erikson, E. (1968). *Identity, Youth and Crisis*. London, Faber.

Farina, A. (1960). 'Patterns of role dominance and conflict in parents of schizophrenic patients', *Journal of Abnormal Social Psychology*, **61**, 31–38.

Fletcher, R. (1966). *The Family and Marriage in Britain*. London, Penguin.

Freedman, N. F. and Hoffman, S. P. (1967). 'Kinetic behaviour in altered clinical states: Approach to objective analysis of motor behaviour during clinical interviews', *Perceptual and Motor Skills*, **24**, 527–539.

Freeman, W. (1950). 'Plane of section in leucotomy in relation to social adjustment', *Congres Internationale de Psychiatrie*, **III**, Paris, Hermann et Cie.

Freud, S. (1917). *Mourning and Melancholia*. 3rd Ed. 1946. London, Hogarth Press.

Friedman, A. S. (1975). 'Interaction of drug therapy with marital therapy in depressive patients', *Archives of General Psychiatry*, **32**, 619–637, Copyright 1975 American Medical Association.

Goldman-Eisler, F. (1958). 'The predictability of words in context and length of pauses in speech', *Language and Speech,* **1,** 226.

Greene, B. I., Lustig, N., and Lee, R. R. (1976). 'Marital therapy when one spouse has a primary affective disorder', *American Journal of Psychiatry,* **133,** 827–830.

Garman, A. S. and Kniskern, D. P. (1977). Research in marital and family therapy. In Gerfield, S. and Bergin, A (Eds.) (1977). *Handbook of Psychotherapy and Behaviour Change,* 2nd Ed. New York, Wiley.

Hagnell, O. and Kreitman, N. (1974). 'Mental illness in married pairs in a total population', *British Journal of Psychiatry,* **125,** 293–302.

Harlow, H. F. (1962). 'The heterosexual affectional system in monkeys', *American Psychologist,* **17,** 1–9.

Haley, J. (1963). *Strategies of Psychotherapy.* New York, Grune and Stratton.

Haley, J. (1972). Critical overview of present status of family interaction research. In J. L. Framo, (Ed.). *Family Interaction.* New York, Springer Publishing Co.

Hinchliffe, M., Hooper, D., Roberts, F. J., and Vaughan, P. W. (1977). 'The melancholy marriage; an enquiry into the interaction of depression. Part II. Expressiveness', *British Journal of Medical Psychology,* **50,** 125–142.

Hinchliffe, M. K., Hooper, D., Roberts, F. J., and Vaughan, P. W. (1978). *The melancholy marriage; an enquiry into the interaction of depression. Part IV. Disruptions',* British Journal of Medical Psycholog,, **51,** 15–24.

Hinchliffe, M. K., Lancashire, M. H.,and Roberts, F. J. (1970). Eye contact and depression: a preliminary report. *British Journal of Psychiatry,* **117,** 571–572.

Hinchliffe, M. K., Lancashire, M. H., and Roberts, F. J. (1971). 'Depression: defence mechanisms in speech', *British Journal of Psychiatry,* **118,** 471–472.

Hinchliffe, M., Vaughan, P. W., Hooper, D., and Roberts, F. J. (1978). 'The melancholy marriage: an enquiry into the interaction of depression. Part III. Responsiveness', *British Journal of Medical Psychology,* **51,** 1–13.

Hinde, R. A. (1956). 'Ethological models and the concept of drive', *British Journal of Philosophy of Science,* **VI,** 311–331.

Hirsch, S. R. and Leff, J. P. (1975). *Abnormalities in the parents of schizophrenics.* Maudsley Monograph No. 22. London, Oxford University Press.

Holmes, T. H. and Rahe, R. H. (1967). 'The social adjustment rating scale', *Journal of Psychosomatic Research,* **11,** 213–218.

Hooper, D., Roberts, F. J., Hinchliffe, M., and Vaughan, P. W. (1977). 'The melancholy marriage: an enquiry into the interaction of depression. Part I Introduction', *British Journal of Medical Psychology,* **50,** 113–124.

Hooper, D. and Sheldon, A. (1969). 'Evaluating newly married couples', *British Journal of Social and Clinical Psychology,* **8,** 169–182.

Hooper, D., Vaughan, P. W., Hinchliffe, M., and Roberts, F. J. (1978). 'The melancholy marriage: an enquiry into the interaction of depression. Part V. Power', *British Journal of Medical Psychology,* In press.

Jackson, D. D. (1968). *Mirages of Marriage.* New York, W. W. Norton.

Klerman, G. L. (1974). Depression and adaption. In R. J. Friedman and M. Katz, (Eds.). *Psychology of Depression: Contemporary Theory and Research.* New York, J. Wiley.

Klerman, G. and DiMascio, A. (1973). 'Long-term treatment of depression with drugs and psychotherapy', *Psychopharmacological Bulletin,* **9,** 55–68.

Knight, M. (1969) 'Bifrontal stereotactic tractotomy: an atraumatic operation of value in the treatment of intense psychoneurosis', *British Journal of Psychiatry,* **115,** 257–266.

Koestler, A. (1964). *Ghost in the Machine.* London, Hutchinson Publishing Group.

Koestler, A. (1949). *Insight and Outlook.* London, Macmillan.

Kreitman, N., Collins, J., Nelson, B., and Troop, J. (1970, 1971). 'Neurosis and marital interaction. I. Personality and Symptoms', *British Journal of Psychiatry,* **117,** 33–46. 'II. Time sharing and social activity', *British Journal of Psychiatry,* **117,** 47–58. 'IV. Manifest psychological interaction', *British Journal of Psychiatry,* **119,** 243–252.

143

Kuhn, T. S. (1962). *The Structure of Scientific Revolutions*. Chicago, University of Chicago Press.

Lazare, A. and Klerman, G. (1968). 'Hysteria and depression: the frequency and significance of hystérical personality features in hospitalized depressed women', *American Journal of Psychiatry*, **124**, 11 May Supp.

Leff, M. J., Roatch, J. F., and Bunney, W. E. (1970). 'Environmental factors preceding the onset of severe depressions', *Psychiatry*, **33**, 293–311.

Levitt, E. E. and Lubin, B. (1975). *Depression: Concepts, Controversies and Some New Facts*. New York, Springer.

Lewin, K, (1948). *Resolving Social Conflicts*. New York, Harper Bros.

Lewinsohn, P. M. and Shaeffer, M. (1971). 'Interpersonal behaviours in the home of depressed versus non-depressed psychiatric and normal controls', *Proceedings of Western Psychology Association*, San Francisco, U.S.A.

Lomas, P. (Ed.) (1967). *The Predicament of the Family*. London, The Hogarth Press.

Mainz, F. (1971). *Foundations of Biology*. Chicago, Chicago University Press.

McPartland, T. S. and Hornstra, R. K. (1964). 'The depressive datum', *Comprehensive Psychiatry*, **5**, 253–261.

Mayer, D. Y. (1975). 'Psychotropic drugs and the "anti-depressed" personality', *British Journal of Medical Psychology*, **48**, 349–357.

McKeown, T. (1976). *The Role of Medicine: Dream, Mirage, or Nemesis*. London, Nuffield Provincial Hospitals Trust.

McLean, P. D., Ogston, K., and Grauer, L. (1973). 'A behavioural approach to the treatment of depression', *Journal of Behavioural Therapy and Experimental Psychiatry*, **4**, 323–330.

McLean, P. (1976). 'Therapeutic decision-making in the behavioural treatment of depression', In P. O. Davidson, (Ed.). *The Behavioural Management of Anxiety Depression and Pain*. New York, Brunner–Mazel.

Mahl, G. F. (1956). 'Disturbances and silences in the patient's speech in psychotherapy', *Journal of Abnormal Social Psychology*, **53**, 1–15.

Mechanic, D. (1968). *Medical Sociology: a Selective View*. New York, Free Press.

Meir, A. Z. (1969). 'General system theory. Developments and perspectives for medicine and psychiatry', *Archives of General Psychiatry*, **21**, 302–310.

Menninger, K. (1963). *The Vital Balance*. New York, Viking Press.

Meyer, A. (1904). 'Report of Proceedings of New York Neurological Society'. *Journal of Nervous and Mental Desease*, **32**, 114–115.

Mills, T. M. (1964). *Group Transformation*. Englewood Cliffs, N. J., Prentice Hall.

Minuchin, S. (1974). *Families and Family Therapy*. Cambridge, Mass, Harvard University Press.

Mishler, E. G. and Waxler, N. (1968). *Interaction in Families*. New York, John Wiley and Sons.

Money, J. and Erhardt, A. A. (1973). *Man and Woman, Boy and Girl*. Baltimore, John Hopkins University Press.

Morgan, H. G., Burns-Cox, C. J., Pocock, H., and Pottle, S. (1975). 'Deliberate self-harm: clinical and socioeconomic characteristics of 368 patients', *British Journal of Psychiatry*, **127**, 564–574.

Mowrer, O. H. (1961). *The Crisis in Psychiatry and Religion*. New York, Van Nostrand.

Ovenstone, I. M. E. (1973). 'The development of neurosis in the wives of neurotic men. Part 1. Symptomatology and personality', *British Journal of Psychiatry*, **122**, 35–47.

Ovenstone, I. M. E. (1973). 'The development of neurosis in the wives of neurotic men. Part 2. Marital role function and marital tensions', *British Journal of Psychiatry*, **122**, 711–717.

Overall, J. (1971). 'Associations between marital history and the nature of manifest psychopathology', *Journal of Abnormal Psychology*, **78**, 213–221.

Parsons, T. and Bales, R. F. (Eds.) (1955). *Family, Socialisation and Interaction Process*. Glencoe, Illinois, Free Press.

Partridge, E. H. (1970). *A Dictionary of Slang and Unconventional English*, 5th Ed. London, Routledge.

Paykel, E., Weissman, M., Prusoff, B. A., and Tonks, C. (1971). 'Dimensions of social adjustment in depressed women', *Journal of Nervous and Mental Disease*, **152**, 158–172.

Paykel, E. S., Myers, J. K., Dienfelt, M. N., and Klerman, G. L. (1969). 'Life events and depression: a controlled study', *Archives of General Psychiatry*, **21**, 753–760.

Pincus, L. (Ed.) (1960). *Marriage: Studies in Emotional Conflict and Growth*. London, Methuen.

Pitt, B. (1968). ' "Atypical" depression following childbirth', *British Journal of Psychiatry*, **114**, 1325–1335.

Polak, P. (1971). 'Social system intervention', *Archives of General Psychiatry*, **25**, 110–117.

Pond, D. A., Ryle, A., and Hamilton, M. (1963). 'Marriage and neurosis in a working class population', *British Journal of Psychiatry*, **109**, 592–598.

Popper, K. (1949). *The Open Society and Its Enemies*. London, Routledge and Kegan Paul.

Porter, A. M. W. (1970). 'Depressive illness in a general practice: a demographic study and controlled trial of Imipramine', *British Medical Journal*, **i**, 773–778.

Rapoport, D. (1960). 'The structure of psychoanalytic theory', *Psychological Issues*, **II**, Monograph No. 6.

Rapoport, R. (1967). The study of marriage as a critical transition for personality and family development. In P. Lomas (Ed.). *The Predicament of the Family*. London. Hogarth Press.

Raush, H., Barry, W. A., Hertel, R. K., and Swain, M. A. (1974). *Communication, Conflict and Marriage*. San Francisco, Jossey–Bass.

Resnich, P. J. (1969). 'Child murder by parents: a psychiatric review of filicide', *America Journal of Psychiatry*, **126**, 325–334.

Roberts, F. J. (1973). *Depression: a Linguistic, Historical, and Philosophical Exploration*. Unpublished M.D. Thesis, Bristol University, Bristol.

Roberts, F. J. (1971). 'Conjoint marital therapy and the prisoner's dilemma', *British Journal of Medical Psychology*, **44**, 67–73.

Roberts, F. J. and Hooper, D. (1969). 'The natural history of attempted suicide in Bristol', *British Journal of Medical Psychology*, **42**, 303–312.

Robertson, N. C. (1974). 'The relationship between marital status and the risk of psychiatric referral', *British Journal of Psychiatry*, **124**, 191–202.

Ruesch, J. and Bateson, G. (1968). *Communication: The Social Matrix of Psychiatry*. New York, Norton.

Rutter, M. (1966). *Children of Sick Parents: an Environmental and Psychiatric Study*. Maudsley Monograph No. 16. London, Oxford University Press.

Rutter, M. (1972). *Maternal Deprivation Reassessed*. London, Penguin Books.

Ryle, A. (1974). *Frames and Cages*. Sussex University Press.

Sager, C. J. (1966). 'The development of marriage therapy; an historical review', *American Journal of Orthopsychiatry*, **36**, 458–467.

Sarbin, T. R. (1964). 'Anxiety: reification of a metaphor', *Archives of General Psychiatry*, **10**, 630–638.

Sarbin, T. R. (1968). 'Ontology recapitulates philology: the mythic nature of anxiety', *American Psychologist*, **23**, 411–418.

Sarbin, T. R. (1969). The Scientific Status of the Mental Illness Metaphor. In Plog, S. and Edgerton, R. B. (Eds.), *Changing Perspectives in Mental Illness*. New York, Holt Rinehart and Winston.

Scanzoni, J. H. (1970). *Opportunity and the Family*. New York, Free Press.

Schaffer, H. R. (1971). *The Growth of Sociability*. London, Penguin Books.

Scheff, T. (1966). *Being Mentally Ill*. Chicago, Aldine Publishing Co.

Schless, A. P. (1974). 'How depressives view the significance of life events', *British Journal of Psychiatry*, **125**, 406–410.

Seligman, M. E. P. (1974). Depression and learned helplessness. In R. J. Friedman and M. Katz, (Eds.). *Psychology of Depression: Contemporary Theory and Research*. New York, John Wiley.

Seligman, M. E. P. (1975). *Helplessness: on Depression, Development, and Death*. San Francisco, W. H. Freeman.

Shands, H. C. and Melzer, J. D. (1973). *Language and Psychiatry*. Hague, Mouton.

Shepherd, M., Cooper, B., Brown, A. C., and Kalton, G. W. (1966). *Psychiatric Illness in General Practice*. London, Oxford University Press.

Shopsin, B. and Kline, M. (1975). In S. Arieti and G. Chrzanowski (Eds.). *New Dimensions in Psychiatry; a World View*. New York, J. Wiley.

Skynner, A. C. R. (1976). *One Flesh: Separate Persons*. London, Constable.

Strodtbeck, F. L. (1951). 'Husband wife interaction over revealed differences', *American Sociol. Review*, **16**, 468–473.

Sullivan, H. S. (1953). *Conceptions of Modern Psychiatry*. London, Tavistock.

Truax, C. B. and Carkhuff, R. R. (1967). *Toward Effective Counseling and Psychotherapy: Training and Practice*. Chicago, Aldine Publishing Company.

Turner, M. B. (1967). *Philosophy and the Science of Behaviour*. New York, Appleton Century and Crofts.

Vaughn, C. E. and Leff, J. P. (1976). 'The influence of family and social factors on the course of psychiatric illness', *British Journal of Psychiatry*, **129**, 125–137.

Walrond-Skinner, S. (1976). *Family Therapy*. London, Routledge and Kegan Paul.

Watzlawick, P., Beavin, J. H., and Jackson, D. D. (1967). *Pragmatics of Human Communication*. New York, W. W. Norton and Co.

Watzlawick, P., Weakland, J., and Fish, R. (1974). *Change: Principles of Problem Formation and Problem Resolution*. New York, W. W. Norton and Co.

Weissman, M. S., and Paykel, E. S. (1974). *The Depressed Woman: a Study of Social Relationships*. Chicago, University of Chicago Press.

Weissman, M. S. and Klerman, G. L. (1977). 'Sex differences and the epidemiology of depression', *Archives of General Psychiatry*, **34**, 98–111.

Winnicott, D. W. (1971). *Therapeutic Consultation in Child Psychiatry*. London, Hogarth Press.

Winokur, G., Clayton, P. J. and Reich, T. (1969). *Manic Depressive Illness*. St. Louis, Mo, C. V. Mosby and Co.

Wynne, L. C. and Singer, M. T. (1963). 'Thought disorder and family relations of schizophrenics. I. A research strategy', *Archives of General Psychiatry*, **9**, 191–198.

Young, M. and Willmott, P. (1975). *The Symmetrical Family*. London, Penguin Books.

Zung, W. W. K. (1965). 'A self-rating depression scale', *Archives of General Psychiatry*, **12**, 63–70.

# INDEX